A STUDENT'S COMPANION FOR

The St. Martin's Guide to Writing

Thirteenth Edition

Wallace T. Cleaves
University of California, Riverside

bedford/st.martin's
Macmillan Learning
Boston | New York

Vice President: Leasa Burton
Program Director, English: Stacey Purviance
Senior Program Manager: Laura Arcari
Director of Content Development: Jane Knetzger
Development Editor: Cara Kaufman
Director of Media Editorial: Adam Whitehurst
Media Editor: Julia Domenicucci
Marketing Manager: Vivian Garcia
Senior Director, Content Management Enhancement: Tracey Kuehn
Senior Managing Editor: Michael Granger
Senior Manager of Publishing Services: Andrea Cava
Senior Content Project Manager: Lidia MacDonald-Carr
Senior Workflow Project Manager: Jennifer Wetzel
Production Coordinator: Brianna Lester
Director of Design, Content Management: Diana Blume
Cover Design: William Boardman
Director of Digital Production: Keri deManigold
Media Project Manager: Allison Hart
Project Management: Lumina Datamatics, Inc.
Senior Project Manager: Aravinda Doss, Lumina Datamatics, Inc.
Editorial Services: Lumina Datamatics, Inc.
Composition: Lumina Datamatics, Inc.
Printing and Binding: LSC Communications

Library of Congress Control Number: 2021934952

ISBN 978-1-319-40878-7

Printed in the United States of America.

1 2 3 4 5 6 26 25 24 23 22 21

For information, write: Bedford/St. Martin's, 75 Arlington Street, Boston, MA 02116

CONTENTS

PART TWO: Writing Activities* 25

* The activities in Chapters 4–12 of this *Student's Companion* supplement activities in the Guides to Reading and Writing in the Writing Activities chapters, in Part 1 of *The St. Martin's Guide to Writing*, Thirteenth Edition.

PART ONE

Succeeding in College

1

Building Your Confidence

Confidence can help drive and shape your experiences as a student, performer, athlete, employee, parent, and the many other roles you play in your life. True confidence is often defined as having a positive and realistic belief about yourself and your talents and traits. *Assertive*, *optimistic*, *eager*, *proud*, *independent*, *trustworthy*, and *mature* are a few terms associated with someone who has true confidence. Conversely, a lack of confidence can result in a poor performance in those same roles.

Here are just a few reasons to develop confidence:

- **Confidence helps sell who you are.** Knowledge, skills, and experience are necessary and important. If you do not possess and project an air of confidence, others may not realize you have these qualities.
- **Confidence reassures others.** It can encourage people in your life to trust you, whether they are your peers, classmates, coworkers, or loved ones.

This guide explores the role that confidence plays in everyday success and offers strategies to build your confidence levels around all of the roles you play in your life.

Not Feeling Confident

Have you had any trouble maintaining your confidence since you started college? It may surprise you to learn that you are not the only first-year student who feels this way. Many students who enter college for the first time feel just like you do: not very certain of all that lies ahead and unsure how to deal with a number of challenges, both in and out of the classroom. Below are just a few steps you can take to help to develop more confidence:

- **Take a strengths inventory.** Make a list of what you're good at.
- **Set measurable, attainable goals.** Ask yourself what you want to accomplish in the next week, month, or year, and then break those goals up into smaller, short-term goals.

- **Take responsibility for your actions.** Make a consistent effort to learn from your experiences (the good and the bad) and own your choices.
- **Dare to take intellectual risks.** Question assumptions, and ask yourself if the things you believe to be true actually are.
- **Examine and acknowledge feelings.** When something bothers you, ask why.
- **Take charge and be persistent.** Remember, luck is 99% perseverance.
- **Assert yourself.** When you want something, you've got to ask.
- **Remember, you're not alone.** Identify individuals who exhibit confidence and make a strong effort to model the types of behavior that make the greatest impression on you.
- **Believe in yourself.**

Identifying Strengths and Setting Goals

Why not start building your confidence by reminding yourself what you are good at? You can start with this simple, yet effective, activity:

Make a list of what you believe are your strongest skills and qualities. Take the time to think deeply and honestly about this exercise before you start. Another way to do this is to ask yourself: "When I feel like I am at my best, what am I doing?" Continue performing those activities to create an increased sense of confidence.

Long-term goals vs. short-term goals: How do they differ? A crucial part of developing, building, and maintaining your confidence is to set long- and short-term goals that you can reach and that will meet your expectations. Think of long-term goals as the final product and short-term goals as the steps along the way. For example, if you were to write a ten-chapter novel, you'd have ten short-term goals (write a chapter) and one long-term goal (write a novel).

THE CONFIDENCE CHECKLIST

Before examining a series of meaningful steps you can take to build confidence, let's start with the following confidence checklist. How would you respond to the following statements? Be as completely truthful and objective as you can be.

	Yes	No
I believe I know what is best for me.	❑	❑
I feel I am a genuine person.	❑	❑
I am extremely tolerant of others in my life.	❑	❑
I am consistent — I do as I say.	❑	❑

	Yes	No
I avoid procrastinating.	❑	❑
I take an active role in classroom discussions.	❑	❑
I have an inner voice that guides my decisions.	❑	❑
I maintain good eye contact and tone of voice when speaking.	❑	❑
I often doubt myself.	❑	❑
I am able to handle constructive criticism.	❑	❑
I have difficulty trusting others.	❑	❑
I often feel awkward in a group.	❑	❑
I would describe myself as an outgoing and assertive individual.	❑	❑
I feel I am capable of assessing my true capabilities.	❑	❑
I am an optimistic person by nature.	❑	❑

If you answered "no" to more than half of the statements, your level of confidence is likely not where you want it to be—and you're probably not alone! Keep reading for some proven strategies to boost your confidence.

Now it's your turn.

- Select one goal you would like to achieve in the next month. Be specific about what that goal is.
- Now identify two or three effective actions you will take to obtain this goal. Once again, be specific and include a time frame for performing these actions.
- Think of one possible barrier that might prevent you from reaching this goal.
- Now consider one action you will take to overcome this barrier. Be sure to detail what this action will be.
- Finally, honestly assess how likely you are to achieve this goal.

TIP

So how does setting goals help build confidence? Think about it this way: If you set up a series of short-term goals you know you can achieve, aren't you going to feel more confident each time you check off one of those goals? Even better, aren't you going to feel like a rock star by the time you achieve your ultimate long-term goal? There is nothing that builds more confidence than seeing hard work pay off.

Learning from Your Experiences and Choices

Wisdom can be gained through both good and bad experiences and through the outcomes of the choices we make. If you can accept that you are ultimately the one responsible for your actions, not others, it is the first important step to practicing this philosophy while in college.

One strategy for maintaining this belief is to not play the blame game; for example, if you received a bad grade, be honest with yourself and ask what role you played in earning the grade. Admitting you are the one responsible for your actions and then responding (and learning) from that outcome will help strengthen your self-esteem and confidence.

Taking Risks

Has anyone ever said, "Nothing ventured, nothing gained" to you? Taking a risk can be an unsettling challenge – you can't be sure it will be worth it, you may question whether you have the ability and the desire to attempt something, and you might think about the what will happen if you are unsuccessful.

Now that's the negative approach. What if you turned this around and, instead, took a chance on something daunting? What if you decided that no matter what obstacles got in your way or what doubts crept into your mind, you would continue to pursue whatever you set out to accomplish? Imagine how you will feel when the results turn out to be positive ones.

Another way of thinking about this is "If you remain in your comfort zone you will not go any further." While taking a risk can seem difficult at first, it almost always pays off in the end – especially in the classroom.

Taking Risks in the Classroom

Your instructors have probably urged you to question rather than to simply accept everything you read or hear. If you follow this advice, you'll take risks in the classroom all the time – intellectual risks, otherwise known as critical thinking. You do this when you speak up in class, when you write an essay, and whenever you carefully rethink long-held beliefs.

Speaking Up in Class

The reward for intellectual risk-taking is that you come away with a better understanding of yourself and the world around you. But what if you are terrified of speaking up in class and of saying something dumb? What if you simply don't know where to start? Below are two case studies to help you start thinking about how to better approach intellectual risks.

Student A read the class material twice and completed all the assignments. She came to class prepared to take notes and was ready and willing to listen to what the instructor had to say on the topic being presented. As an adult student, she was used to participating in meetings at work, and she didn't feel nervous about speaking up, so she didn't think that she needed to prepare any additional material.

Student B also completed the assigned homework and believed he knew the material. He also knew he would be reluctant to share his thoughts or respond to questions posed to the class. As a strategy, he wrote down several questions and responses to what he assumed would be a part of the class discussion. When he attended class, he referred to his list of questions and answers when those areas of discussion came up.

What strategies did each student employ that would help them take intellectual risks? Who do you think came to class better prepared? For each case study, what would you recommend the student do differently next time?

Exercise: Questions and Answers

What do you do to prepare for class discussions? Both Student A and Student B are good students. They read the material and did their assignments. Student B, however, uses higher-level thinking questions to help stimulate critical thinking. As you prepare for class, try to use the following generic question stems to ask questions about the material covered. Then take a few minutes to jot down your answers.

What would happen if ___________?

What is the difference between ___________ and ___________?

What are the implications of ___________?

Why is ___________ important?

What is another way to look at ___________?

Examining Emotions

Daniel Goleman, author and creator of the theory of emotional intelligence (EQ), stresses the vital role EQ plays in building self-confidence. One of his key components is Emotional Self-Management, or the ability to make sensible decisions even when your emotions tell you to do otherwise. For example, if you received a failing grade on a quiz, your first impulse might be to get angry. Even worse, you might consider dropping the class. A better strategy would be to examine why you earned the grade and allow yourself the time needed to learn how to succeed in the course. Examining your feelings and how you react to certain situations can keep you from giving up too early on something that is challenging.

Exercise: What Makes a Success?

Make a list of the qualities you see in people you think of as confident. Share the list with someone else in your class and discuss which of these qualities have to do with feelings and interactions with other people. How many of these qualities do you see in yourself?

Being Persistent

One of the simplest ways to gain confidence is to be persistent. *Persistence* simply means the ability to stick with something through completion, even if you don't always want to. If a task or challenge seems difficult at times and the outcome may be uncertain, persistence helps you keep at it. Let's look at an example:

Imagine that you are frustrated with the teaching style of one of your instructors. She presents the material in a way that doesn't work for you (but it seems to for your classmates). You can elect to drop the class early in the semester and perhaps have a different teacher next time, or you could take steps that will allow you to persist in the course, such as working with a tutor, forming a study group, or meeting with your professor for clarification. In the end, you will not have given up and your outcome could be a favorable one.

ASSERTIVENESS CHECK-UP

Answer the following questions as honestly as you can:

- Do you express your point of view even when it is not the same as others?
- Will you actually say "no" to a request made by friends or coworkers that you feel is unreasonable?
- How easily do you accept constructive criticism?
- Are you willing to ask for help?
- Do you make decisions or judgments with confidence?
- How open are you to another person's suggestions or advice?
- When you state your thoughts or feelings, do you do so in a direct and sincere manner?
- Are you likely to cooperate with others to achieve a worthwhile goal?

Ultimately, it is *your* responsibility to take charge of your success and persist—even if you have some setbacks at first. When you feel like you may be about to give up, remind yourself of your long-term goals and how persisting at the current task will help you attain those goals.

Being Assertive

One of the best ways to build confidence is to let people know what you want and don't want, how you feel, and when you need help. The more skilled you are at letting people know these things, the more assertive you'll become. The more you *successfully* assert yourself, the more confident you'll become. So how do you become more assertive? Let's start by assessing where you are right now.

If you answered "yes" to less than half of the questions in the "Assertiveness Check-Up" box above, the strategies below can help you feel more confident when you are attempting to be assertive.

- Use suitable facial expressions.
- Always maintain good eye contact.
- Watch your tone of voice. Your voice should be firm, audible, and pleasant.
- Be aware of your body language—how you stand, sit, and gesture.
- Actively listen to others so that you can accurately confirm what they have said.
- Ask reasoned questions when something is unclear to you.
- Take a win-win approach to solving problems: How can what you're asking for benefit both you and the person you're asking?

Developing a Network

When you create a supportive network of individuals, you are being interdependent, and this is a key to fostering self-confidence. By building mutually helpful relationships you are more likely to achieve your goals and dreams. Here are some strategies for developing this interdependence:

- Actively seek out your school's many resources. This will mean connecting with an academic advisor, signing up for a tutor if you need one, or getting involved with several on- or off-campus activities.
- Foster a valuable relationship with your instructors; ask for their assistance, feedback, and constructive criticism.
- Start a study group by looking for several classmates who are prepared, regularly attend classes, and take an active part in class discussions. Don't overlook a quiet student who may have true insight into the course; he or she can prove an asset. Approach those you've identified and suggest forming the group. If the answer is yes, decide on your group's mutual goals and the rules your group will follow.
- Coming to college can be a challenging and emotionally stressful experience; fortunately, your school offers counselors who can provide the understanding and skills to help you overcome what's in your way. Turning to one can be the right thing to do.

Getting Advice from Other Students

The Goal Setter: Liberal Arts Major at the Community College of Rhode Island

Having little idea what he wanted to do upon entering college, The Goal Setter elected to not declare a specific major; instead he chose general education courses to slowly get himself "into the student mindset." High school had been a struggle academically and personally, so a four-year school was not an immediate option. Previously, his only goal was to not leave school early, and now he realized he needed more structure. He connected with an advisor, and she suggested that he first take a self-assessment test and come up with a set of both short-term and long-term goals, based on the results. The advisor explained the value of the exercise and cautioned against giving up before achieving some or all of those goals. The Goal Setter heeded this advice, earned his associate's degree, and has since transferred to a four-year college, full of confidence that his next goal of a bachelor's diploma will be realized.

The Networker: Marketing Major at Bryant University, Rhode Island

Her high school counselor told The Networker that she was "not college material" and she retained that belief until her early thirties, when she decided that she had something to prove to the counselor *and to herself.* She employed interdependence, surrounding herself with students who practiced successful strategies and who regularly encouraged her. The result was a mostly successful first-semester experience. Following this positive outcome, she never looked back. She anticipated the day when she would return to her former high school to show her diploma to her former guidance counselor.

TIPS FOR CONFIDENCE BUILDING

Here are some time-tested strategies that will help you throughout your life. By following these steps, you will achieve *realistic and worthwhile* confidence:

- As often as possible, focus on your strong points rather than areas of weakness. In other words, be aware of what is good about you rather than what you are not proud of.
- Make a consistent effort to learn from your experiences — the good and bad (you will undoubtedly have many of both in your life).
- Find the courage to try something new and different, even when it appears too difficult or risky.
- When something bothers or disappoints you, take the time to examine your thoughts. Choose to react calmly and rationally rather than impulsively and emotionally.
- Expect that while some of what you achieve in life may be due to pure luck, a good deal more will likely be the result of your personal persistence and effort.
- Strive to be assertive. This means express how you feel, what you think, the beliefs you hold, and do so directly and sincerely. You have a right to say "no" to requests that are not genuine or reasonable.
- Continue to learn and vary your skills and talents long after you leave college. Embrace the idea that there is no end to learning throughout your life.
- Most important of all, believe in yourself. Identify what distinguishes you from everyone else and what you have to offer. Once you know these qualities, you will begin to cultivate them by applying them in everyday life.

2

Managing Your Time

You might be the kind of student who thinks it's normal to spend hours making flashcards and outlining your notes in different colored ink. Or maybe you're an adrenaline junkie, accustomed to starting a twenty-page term paper the night before it's due.

The problem is both of these approaches carry certain inherent liabilities. Goof off and you'll probably bomb all your courses. Do nothing but cower in a library carrel for weeks on end and you'll wind up dull, pasty, and miserable. If you're like most of us, you'll learn more, get better grades, and have more fun in college if you operate somewhere in the middle.

By now, you've probably heard the Latin expression *carpe diem,* which translates to "seize the day" (as in, make time work for you). Mastering the art of time management is one key to your future success and happiness, but learning to actually make time work for you can be problematic. What can you do to take control of your own time?

The Case for Time Management

Why bother? We know. Some students don't want to "waste" time on planning and managing their schedules. Instead, they prefer to go with the flow. Unfortunately, the demands of college (not to mention most careers) require serious, intentional strategies. Unless you can afford to hire a personal assistant, your previous slacker habits won't carry you through.

To psych yourself up, think of time management as part of your life skill set. If you're trying to remember all the things you need to get done, it's hard to focus on actually doing the work. Organizing your time well accomplishes three things: First, it optimizes your chances for good results, so you're not flying by the seat of your pants. Second, it enhances your life by saving you from stress and regret. And finally, it reflects what you value—it's all about doing your best.

Need more motivation? Remember that people who learn good time management techniques in college generally soar in their careers. Think about it: If you're more efficient at your job, you'll be able to accomplish more. That will give you a competitive advantage over your coworkers. Your bosses will learn to depend on you. They'll reward you with interesting projects, promotions, and educational and training opportunities. You'll feel empowered and will fill your workplace with positive vibes. You'll have time for a sizzling social life outside the office. Plus you'll make more money and need less Red Bull.

Taking Charge of Your Time

Freedom can be a dangerous thing. One of the biggest differences between high school and college is that you find yourself with far more independence – and greater responsibility – than you've ever known. If you are continuing your education after a break, you may also be contending with spouse/boss/child obligations, too. But it would be a gigantic mistake to assume that Oprah, rocket scientists, and other type-A folks have some kind of monopoly on organization and focus. You, the ordinary student, can also embrace your inner executive assistant – the one who keeps you on time, on task, and ready for a slice of the action. So how do you begin?

Setting Goals

Goals help you figure out where to devote the majority of your time. To achieve your goals, you need to do more than just think about them: You need to act! This action requires setting some short-term and long-term goals. When determining your long-term goals, it is important to be honest and realistic with yourself. Goals should be challenging, but they should also be attainable. Be sure they align with your abilities, values, and interests. Do you want to go on to further schooling? Have you decided what career you want to pursue? Mulling over these questions can help you start thinking about where you want to be in the next 5 to 10 years. Dreaming up long-term goals can be exciting and fun; however, reaching your goals requires undertaking a number of steps in the short term.

Try to be very specific when determining your short-term goals. For example, if you're committed to becoming an expert in a certain field, you'll want to throw yourself into every class and internship that can help you on your way. A specific goal would be to review your school's course catalog, identify the courses you want to take, and determine when you must take them. An even more specific goal would be to research interesting internship opportunities in your field of study. The good news about goals is that each small step adds up.

Identify one long-term goal and list three steps you can take to achieve your goal.

Long-Term Goal ______________________________

Steps toward Your Goal

1. ______________________________
2. ______________________________
3. ______________________________

Knowing Your Priorities

Prioritize your life so that you're steadily working toward achieving your goals.

- **Start out with a winner's mentality:** Make sure your studies take precedence. Having worked so hard to get to college, you cannot allow other activities to derail your schoolwork. Review your current commitments and prepare to sacrifice a few – for now. Whatever you do, talk to your family, your boss, and your friends about your college workload and goals so that everyone's on the same page. When you have a looming deadline, be firm. Emphasize that no amount of badgering will succeed in getting you to go to the superhero theme party during finals week.
- **Next, start preparing for your future:** Visit your campus career center and schedule an assessment test to hone in on your talents and interests. Or, if you know what career you want to pursue, talk with a professional in that field, your guidance counselor, a professor, or an upper-class student in your chosen major to find out what steps you need to take to get the results you want, starting now. What skills and experiences should be on your résumé when you graduate to make you stand out from the pack? Make a plan, prioritize your goals, and then make a time-management schedule.
- **Balance is key:** If you're realistic, planning for the future you want may demand big sacrifices. Be realistic about the present, too. Always include time in your schedule for people who are important to you and time on your own to recharge.

Embrace the 2-for-1 Rule. For every hour you spend in class at college, you should plan to study two hours more outside of class. That's the standard, so keep it in mind when you're planning your schedule. The bottom line is that you simply carry more responsibility for your education in college than you did in high school.

Own Your Class Schedule. Your schedule will impact almost every aspect of your college life. Before you register, think about how to make your schedule work for you.

> **TIP**
>
> **Share your Google or Outlook Calendar.** Keeping an electronic copy of your calendar allows you to share with others at a click of the button. Letting your family, friends, and employer know what is on your plate at any given moment can bridge any misunderstandings that may arise because of your school commitments and create more supportive home and work environments.

- **Start with your biorhythms.** Do you study more effectively in the day or the evening or a combination of both? Ideally, you should devote your peak hours – when you're most alert and engaged – to schoolwork. Schedule other activities, like laundry, e-mail, exercise, and socializing, for times when it's harder to concentrate.
- **If you live on campus,** you might want to create a schedule that situates you near a dining hall at mealtimes or lets you spend breaks between classes at the library. Feel free to slot breaks for relaxation and catching up with friends. But beware the midday nap: You risk feeling lethargic afterward or, even worse, oversleeping and missing the rest of your classes. If you attend a large college or university, be sure to allow adequate time to get from one class to another.

- **Try to alternate classes with free periods.** Also, seek out instructors who'll let you attend lectures at alternate times in case you're absent. If they offer flexibility with due dates for assignments, all the better.
- **If you're a commuter student or carry a heavy workload,** you might be tempted to schedule your classes in blocks without breaks. But before you do this, consider the following:
  - Falling behind in all your classes if you get sick
  - The fatigue factor
  - No last-minute study periods before tests
  - The possibility of having several exams on the same day

CONTROL FACTOR: KNOW WHAT YOU *CAN* AND *CAN'T* CONTROL

When it comes to planning your time between what you can and can't control, it helps to know the difference.

What You *Can* Control

- **Making good choices.** How often do you say, "I don't have time"? Probably a lot. But truth be told, you have a choice when it comes to most of the major commitments in your life. You also control many of the small decisions that keep you focused on your goals: when you wake up, how much sleep you get, what you eat, how much time you spend studying, and whether you get exercise. So be a woman or man with a plan. If you want something enough, you'll make time for it.
- **Doing your part to succeed.** Translation: Go to all your classes; arrive on time; get all the required textbooks; keep track of your activities; complete every reading and writing assignment on time; take notes in class; and, whenever possible, participate and ask questions.
- **Managing your stress levels.** Organization is the key to tranquility and positive thinking. Manage your time well, and you won't be tormented with thoughts of all the things that need doing. Psychologists have found that free-floating anxiety can turn even your subconscious thoughts into a horror show. Want to avoid unnecessary stress? Plan ahead.

What You *Can't* Control

- **Knowing how much you'll need to study right off the bat.** Depending on the kind of high school you went to (and the types of courses you took there), or if it has been a while since you've had to study, you might be more or less prepared than your college classmates. If your studying or writing skills lag behind, expect to put in a little extra time until you're up to speed.
- **Running into scheduling conflicts.** If you find it hard to get the classes you need, you can seek help from a dean, an academic adviser, or someone in the college counseling center.
- **Needing a job to help pay your way.** Just follow the experts' rule of thumb: If you're taking a full courseload, do your best to avoid working more than fifteen hours a week. Any more than that and your academic work could suffer.

Four Time-Wasting Habits to Avoid

1. Procrastinating

Should you have to do assignments that seem incredibly long and boring? Shouldn't you be able to study with family members in the room, even if you can't get any work done with them around? Can't you occasionally blow off the outside reading? Yes, no, and no.

There are lots of reasons why we procrastinate. Maybe you're a perfectionist – in which case, avoiding a task might be easier than having to live up to your own very high expectations (or those of your parents or instructors). Maybe you object to the sheer dullness of an assignment, or you think you can learn the material just as well without doing the work. Maybe you even fear success and know just how to subvert it.

None of these qualify as valid reasons to put off your work. They're just lame excuses that will get you in trouble. Fortunately, doing tasks you don't like is excellent practice for real life.

Slacker alert: Procrastination is a slippery slope. Research shows that procrastinators are more likely to develop unhealthy habits like higher alcohol consumption, smoking, insomnia, poor diet, and lack of exercise. Make sure you get these tendencies under control early. Otherwise, you could feel overwhelmed in other aspects of your life, too.

Easy Tricks to Stop Procrastination

- *Break big jobs down into smaller chunks.* Spend only a few minutes planning your strategy and then act on it.
- *Find a quiet, comfortable place to work* that doesn't allow for distractions or interruptions. Don't listen to music, and turn off your phone. Shut the door to your room while studying.
- *Treat your study time like a serious commitment.* That means no phone calls, e-mail, text messages, or updates to your social media page. You can rejoin society later.
- *Consider the consequences if you don't get down to work.* You don't want to let bad habits derail your ability to achieve good results *and* have a life.
- *Reward yourself* for finishing the task: Watch your favorite YouTuber or play a game with your kids or friends.

2. Overextending Yourself

Feeling overextended is a huge source of stress for college students. Why? Well, what constitutes a realistic workload varies significantly from one person to another. Being involved in campus life is fun and important; it's crucial not to let your academic work take a back seat.

- **Learn to say no – even if it means letting other people down.** Don't be tempted to compromise your priorities.
- **But don't give up all nonacademic pursuits.** On the contrary, students who work or participate in extracurricular activities often achieve higher grades than

their less-active counterparts partly because time management plays such an important role in their lives.

- **If you're truly overloaded with commitments and can't see a way out,** you may need to drop a course before the drop deadline. It may seem drastic, but a low grade on your permanent record is even worse. Become familiar with your school's add/drop policy to avoid penalties. If you receive financial aid, keep in mind that in most cases you must be registered for a minimum number of credit hours to be considered a full-time student and maintain your current level of aid. Be sure before you drop!

3. Losing Your Focus

Too many first-year college students lose sight of their goals. Translation: They spend their first term blowing off classes and assignments, then either get expelled, placed on probation, or have to spend years clawing their way back to a decent GPA. So plan your strategy and keep yourself motivated for the long haul.

4. Running Late

Punctuality is a virtue. Rolling in late to class or review sessions shows a lack of respect for both your instructors and your classmates. Arrive early and avoid using your phone in class, texting, doing homework for another class, falling asleep, talking, whispering, or leaving class to feed a parking meter. Part of managing your time is freeing yourself to focus on the present and on other people who inhabit the present with you. Note: Respecting others is a habit that can work wonders in your career and personal life.

> **TIP**
>
> **Social Media Addict?** Online tools like *StayFocused* allow you to block or limit your time on certain websites while you are studying so you can focus on the task at hand. Google "10 Online Tools for Better Attention & Focus" to find a program that works for you.

Two Indispensable Tools to Keep You on Track

Here's the deal. Once you enter college or the working world, you must immediately do the following: Write down everything you need to do; prioritize your tasks; and leave yourself constant reminders. The good news is that a little up-front planning will make your life infinitely easier and more relaxing. For one thing, you'll be less likely to screw up. On top of that, you'll free your brain from having to remember all the things you need to get done so you can actually do the work. Two key items will help you plan to succeed: a planner or calendar and a to-do list.

A Planner or Calendar

Find out if your college sells a special planner in the campus bookstore with important dates and deadlines already marked. Or use an online calendar or the one that comes on your computer or smartphone. As you schedule your time, follow a few basic guidelines.

Pick a timeframe that works best for you. If you want a "big picture" sense of how your schedule plays out, try setting up a calendar for the whole term or for the month. For a more detailed breakdown of what you need to accomplish in the near future, a calendar for the week or even the day may be a better fit. Of course, there's no need to limit yourself—use more than one type of calendar if that works for you.

Enter all of your commitments. Once you've selected your preferred timeframe, it's time to record your commitments and other important deadlines. These might include your classes, assignment due dates, work hours, family commitments, and so on. Be specific. For instance, "Read Chapter 8 in history" is preferable to "Study history," which is better than simply "Study." To be even more specific, include meeting times and locations, social events, and study time for each class you're taking. Take advantage of your smartphone and set reminders and alarms to help keep you on top of all your activities and obligations.

Break large assignments like term papers into smaller bits, such as choosing a topic, doing research, creating an outline, learning necessary computer skills, writing a first draft, and so on. And give them deadlines. Estimate how much time each assignment will take you, then get a jump on it. A good time manager often finishes projects before the actual due dates in case there is an emergency.

Watch out for your toughest weeks during the term. If you find that paper deadlines and test dates fall during the same week or even the same day, you can alleviate some stress by finding time to finish some assignments early to free up study and writing time. If there's a major conflict, talk it over with your professor and find a way to work around it. Professors will be more likely to help you if you come to them well in advance of the deadline.

Update your planner/calendar regularly. Enter all due dates as soon as you know them. Be obsessive about this.

Check your planner/calendar every day (at the same time of day if that helps you remember). You'll want to review the current week and the next week, too.

When in doubt, turn to a type-A classmate for advice. A hyper-organized friend can be your biggest ally when it comes to making a game plan.

A To-Do List

The easiest way to remember all the things you need to do is to jot them down in a running to-do list, and keep it updated. You can do this on paper or use an online calendar or smartphone to record the day's obligations. Techies love the GTD® ("Getting Things Done"®) system for taking control of tasks and commitments. Google it to learn how it works.

1. **Prioritize.** Rank items on your list in order of importance. Alternately, circle or highlight urgent tasks. Use exclamation points and stars – it's all good.
2. **Every time you complete a task, cross it off the list.** (It can be extremely satisfying.)

3. **Move items that are not done to the top of your next list.** (Less satisfying, but smart and efficient.)
4. **Start a new to-do list every day or once a week.** It shouldn't be just about academics. Slot in errands you need to run, appointments, e-mail messages you need to send, and anything else you need to do that day or week.

Advice from Other Students

Martha Flot

Education Major in Florida

"I learned a long time ago that if I don't start my work early, it's not going to happen. I always open my books right after the kids are off to school, and begin with the easiest assignments. I feel really productive and get into the swing of things before tackling the harder stuff. It's kind of like the warm-up before practice."

- **Digitally bolster your memory.** "I keep everything in my smartphone calendar. For me, that's the best way to stay organized. I set reminders for all of my study groups and upcoming assignments. If it's a big exam, I'll set the reminder a week in advance to give myself plenty of time to prepare."
- **Exercise.** "I always try to exercise before I sit down for an exam or a long study session, too. Studies show that exercise boosts your blood circulation, so you can think better and feel more awake. For me, it makes a huge difference."
- **Beware of over-committing.** "I used to be a huge people pleaser. Trying to please everyone and juggling my role as a mother, wife, and student, I learned fast that I couldn't do that and still get all my work done. Once I started prioritizing, my friends and family have been responsive and supportive. It helps having a husband who manages his time well; you grow and learn from it."

EASY WAYS TO MAXIMIZE YOUR TIME

- **Carry work with you.** If you have a lull between classes, use it to review material from the previous class and prepare for the next one. Take advantage of waiting time (on the bus or between appointments) to study. You'll be more likely to remember what you've learned in class if you review or copy your notes as soon as you reasonably can.
- **Discipline yourself with routines.** You might want to get up early to prepare, or set fixed study hours after dinner or on weekend afternoons.
- **Don't multitask.** Even though you might be quite good at it — or think you are — research shows that you'll be able to do your most effective studying and retain the most information if you concentrate on one task at a time.
- **Study with friends.** You can help each other grasp tricky concepts and memorize important facts and dates.
- **Be flexible.** Disruptions to your plans don't come with ample warning time. Build extra time into your schedule so that unanticipated interruptions don't prevent you from meeting your goals.

John Dietz

Architecture Major in Florida

"My first two years of college forced me to be a morning person. But as an upperclassman, I have the freedom to pick classes that start in the afternoon, so I've reverted to being nocturnal: I usually study or work in my design studio until 2 or 3 a.m."

- **Go digital.** "I take my computer to all my classes, so I keep a detailed calendar there. My work schedule changes frequently, so I always type that in along with all my assignments."
- **Beware of perfectionism.** "As an architect, you could spend your whole life designing something. Often I really have to tell myself to stop and go on to the next thing."
- **Find a part-time job that offers flexible hours and lets you study.** "I work at the gym on campus, where each shift is just three hours long. They only hire students, so they're very accommodating if I need to change my schedule. Plus, mostly I get to sit at the check-in desk and review my notes."

Carolina Buckler

Business and Political Science Major in Indiana

"Having a double major means a heavier workload, but it's doable in my subjects. My roommate – who's studying engineering and puts in a lot more hours than I do – couldn't have handled a heavier workload because of his major."

- **Start things sooner rather than later.** "That especially helps with group projects because it's hard to find time in everyone's schedule to get together. If you meet early, you can divide up the work."
- **Make sure your employer knows your academic commitments.** "I work twelve to fifteen hours a week as a teacher's assistant in the political science department. The professors will automatically understand if I need to take a study day. Around finals, they give everyone a week off."
- **Socialize at mealtimes.** "My friends and I meet for dinner at 5 p.m. It sounds ridiculously early, but I've found that it makes me less likely to waste time: Instead of trying to start something for an hour or so before dinner, I get back around 6:30 and jump right into homework."

3

Writing Ethically and Responsibly

Thanks to technology, it's easier than ever for students to cheat, so cheaters are sprouting like mushrooms. Thanks to technology, it's also much easier for colleges to catch cheaters. Administrators are cracking down on cheating by making the penalties increasingly harsh.

To complicate matters, there are plenty of students who cheat *without even knowing that they're cheating.* Of course, in a perfect world, they'd get lighter sentences than the people who cheated intentionally. But colleges aren't perfect worlds. They're wonderful institutions of learning that don't like to be taken advantage of.

So let's clear a few things up.

Defining "Cheating"

Cheating comes down to two things: Faking your own work, and helping other students fake theirs.

Some of the Most Obvious Forms of Cheating

- Buying an essay
- Texting answers during an exam
- Sharing the details of a test with students who haven't taken it yet
- Copying someone else's homework
- Peeking at someone else's test paper
- Letting other people cheat off you
- Stealing a test
- Writing answers to the test in crazy small letters on your gum wrappers or on the inside of your bottled water label. (Note: Professors are onto these tricks.)
- Plagiarizing: The most common form of cheating

The trouble with plagiarism is that a lot of students don't completely understand what it is. Plagiarism is a fancy word that, according to the *Oxford English Dictionary,* means "taking someone else's work or ideas and passing them off as one's own." Fun fact: The word *plagiarism* comes from the Latin word for *kidnapping*. Get the picture?

It's hard to believe that anybody *really* thinks it's OK to cut and paste whole sentences from the Internet into their essays. But given that some people don't think twice about downloading copyrighted music tracks and videos, maybe the concept of "borrowing" isn't as clear as it used to be. What's your stance? Have you ever lifted passages off a website, maybe even changing a couple of words to make it sound more like you? Are you inclined to believe that once something is on the web, it's public domain? If so, please know it's NOT so. The fact remains that copying or paraphrasing anything from the Internet, or from any another source, and using it without citing the source is cheating.

Beware: Plagiarizing with intent is one thing. Many college students plagiarize by accident. They copy quotations into their notes but forget to add quotation marks and later can't tell what's their own writing and what they borrowed from a source. These students are also convicted of plagiarism simply because they forget to indicate which parts of their essay are their own and which parts belong to another author. Remember: Colleges are on a crusade to thwart cheating. If your high school was lax about footnotes or paraphrasing, you need to figure out the rules fast.

The Cheating Problem

In a recent survey of 36,000 high school students by the Josephson Institute of Ethics, 60 percent admitted to cheating on a test during the previous year. Thirty-five percent had cheated on multiple tests. A third of them had committed plagiarism, cutting and pasting from the Internet. What's worse, according to recent studies by Donald L. McCabe at Rutgers University, the number of students who think that copying material from the web is "serious cheating" has plummeted to only 29 percent.

Cheating typically begins during junior high, which is – no surprise – around the same time that grade pressure and academic workloads ramp up. In college, the pressure to get good grades becomes even more intense. Maybe you're trying to get into a competitive graduate program, win a scholarship, or land a high-paying job. Maybe you're involved in a zillion clubs, sports, or volunteer activities. Maybe you have a job and/or kids. Maybe you're taking metaphysics. Whatever it is, if you start to feel overextended, you might start to justify cheating in your mind. Big mistake.

Why You Shouldn't Cheat

Because it's wrong. Because it's lazy and contemptible. Because getting caught could set off a firestorm and totally screw up your future. Because cheating is bad for your self-image and can trigger severe guilt and anxiety.

Because attending college is ultimately about learning new things, challenging yourself, and building your integrity. If you try to scam your way through, you've defeated the whole point of this exercise.

And here's the real drag: Cheating has a nasty way of seeping into other parts of your life, like your career, your finances, and your personal relationships, where it can cause long-term damage. Once you've cheated on a few tests, it might not seem like a big deal to pad your résumé or fudge your taxes.

Why It's Easy to Get Caught

College professors have more time and leeway to investigate their suspicions and better resources to back them up. Programs like Turnitin.com let instructors scan essays and crosscheck them against books, newspapers, journals, and student papers, as well as against material that's publicly accessible on the web. Even a tiny, nine-word snippet could give you away.

How *Not* to Cheat: Ten Essential Tips

1. **Avoid friends who pressure you to bend the rules.** Writing a paper is really hard. Doing advanced math and science homework is really hard. Studying for exams is lonely, boring, and *really* hard. But trying to beat the system doesn't pay. Remind yourself of the consequences of cheating. Explain to your friends that you are on a valiant quest for honest effort. Make them watch a lot of movies about Abraham Lincoln. As a last resort, find new friends.
2. **Join a study group.** If you're struggling to get through a daunting course, get together with other students to compare notes and help each other grasp tricky concepts. A study group gives you a support system and a more positive belief in yourself. It teaches you persistence and discipline because the group structure involves meeting promptly at set times for reviews. A study group can also make

THE PENALTIES FOR CHEATING

Cheating is a much bigger deal in college than it was in high school. Remember, you're not a minor anymore. Once you're over 18 and are caught cheating, you'll be reprimanded as an adult.

- "At minimum, you're looking at an F for the entire course and very likely academic probation or even dismissal," says Dr. Thomas Skouras, a professor at the Community College of Rhode Island. "In most cases now, instructors have to adhere to the school's policy on cheating, so they can't bend the rules even if they want to."
- And it gets scarier than that: If caught cheating, you could end up with a Conviction of Plagiarism on your college transcript. That's the same transcript you'll need to use for graduate school and job applications.
- Plagiarism is different from other student offenses in that it isn't protected under federal confidentiality laws. Think about it: "A student who has stalked someone on campus and has a history of psychiatric illness might not have that information on his transcript," Prof. Skouras adds. "A conviction of cheating is much harder to suppress."

Note: How often are convictions of plagiarism overturned? Almost never. Most instructors won't go forward with the charges unless they have substantial evidence to back them up.

learning easier and more fun. Other members of the group may have noticed important points from class that you didn't catch. Plus, once you understand the material well, any impulse to cheat will cease to be an issue.

3. **Don't procrastinate.** Here's the deal: If you want to write a thorough and honest essay, you need to start early. College papers aren't like movie reviews. You're required to do lots of outside research. Then you have to weed through it all to figure out what's valuable. Next, you have to incorporate the highlights into an outline, a first draft, and ultimately, an original, dazzlingly brilliant work that's all your own. All of that takes time. If you leave things too late, you'll be more tempted to cheat.

> TIP
>
> **Make a pledge to successfully pass the course as a team — the honest way.** "I chose to form a group more than a decade ago with three other doctoral candidates and we followed through on our promise to graduate together," says Prof. Skouras. "It really mattered that we were each rooting for the others to succeed."

4. **Don't muddle your notes.** It's vital that you keep your own writing separate from the material you've gathered from other sources. Why? Because it's surprisingly easy to mistake someone else's words for your own, especially after you get two hours into writing and your brain turns numb. So document everything. Be obsessive about this.

5. **Be a stickler for in-text citations.** It happens all the time: At the end of an essay, a student provides a full listing of all the works he or she has cited. But in the paper itself, there are no references to be found. "In this case, you're looking at a low C at best," says Prof. Skouras. "Your instructor has no choice but to take off major points since it's impossible to tell the difference between your writing and your references."

6. **Familiarize yourself with the proper formatting for a research paper.** MLA style is pretty much standard for papers in literature and writing courses. If your instructors require a different style, they will let you know. If you need to learn the basic guidelines and rules for citations, The Online Writing Lab (or OWL) at Purdue University is a great source. It's well written and user-friendly (**owl.english.purdue.edu**). You might also want to speak to a reference librarian. A reference librarian has a graduate degree in gathering research and can be one of your biggest allies in college. Alternately, pay a visit to the writing center on campus or talk to your instructor for advice. Many college libraries offer tutorials in MLA formatting. Getting one early in the semester can give you a big leg up.

> TIP
>
> **Respect deadlines.** When you were in high school, your teachers might have negotiated due dates. In college, it's almost impossible to get an extension on an assignment. Your old stalling tactics ("My printer broke/I have the flu/I've been working with NASA on a nuclear laser shield — so can I get that essay to you on Monday?") won't fly.

> TIP
>
> **Flaunt your knowledge.** Don't just list the references you've used to research your topic; show that you know where they belong in your narrative.

7. **Be sure to list all of your research sources.** If you're not sure how to list a citation or if you're not sure that your source is valid, don't just put it down and keep your fingers crossed. Talk to your instructor, or ask a reference librarian for help.
8. **Master the art of paraphrasing.** Paraphrasing means restating someone else's ideas or observations in your own words and sentences. You don't have to put the text in quotation marks, but a citation acknowledging the original source is still needed. (See *The Rules of Paraphrasing* below for examples.)
9. **If you need help, seek it early.** This sounds painfully obvious, but it's important to go to the writing center or the librarian *well before your paper is actually due.* Revision takes time—and chances are, your paper will need more than a few tweaks.
10. **If you hand something in and then realize that you used material without giving credit to the source, alert your instructor immediately.** Don't just hope it will slip through. Better to risk half a grade on one essay than your whole college career, right?

TIP

When copying research material into your notes, write the name of its source and page number directly after it. Likewise, when you copy something from the Internet, add a URL in brackets at the end. Use quotation marks around all cited materials. You might also try highlighting your research in a bright color to set it apart from your notes. All of this will make things easier when it's time to make your footnotes.

The Rules of Paraphrasing

Paraphrasing doesn't mean copying a quote and swapping out a few words. It doesn't mean changing two or three words in a sequence, either. It means rephrasing someone else's quote altogether while retaining its essential meaning. Consider these examples:

- If the quote is "The likelihood of an increase in the growth rate appears dim," you might change it to "The economy improving in the near future is improbable, according to Dr. X, an economist at the University of Y."
- Likewise, "Google has been working to build cars that can drive themselves," could be rewritten as "One of Google's latest projects: a robotic car that takes humans out of the driver's seat."

If you're having trouble paraphrasing something, try this trick: Put away your source material, call up a friend or your mom, and explain the point you're trying to summarize. Chances are you'll come away with something that's clear, concise, and in your own words.

A word of warning: When you paraphrase someone else's opinions or insights, you still have to document the source. The upside? You don't have to frame the passage in quotation marks.

PART TWO

Writing Activities

4

Autobiography and Literacy Narratives*

Narratives about significant and memorable experiences or events share three basic features:

- They present a well-told story.
- They include vivid descriptions of people and places.
- They highlight the autobiographical significance of the experience or event.

Readings in *The St. Martin's Guide to Writing* provide effective examples that you can refer to as you reflect on and write an autobiography or literacy narrative. Activities in *The Guide* can give you a jumping-off point for your own writing. The activities below provide extra support for reading the autobiography or literacy narratives as a writer, applying what you learn to your own draft, and revising the draft to create a meaningful narrative of your own.

A Well-Told Story

Charting the Dramatic Arc, and Recognizing the Story's Structure

1. Choose one of the readings from Chapter 2 of *The St. Martin's Guide* or a reading your instructor has assigned.† Using Figure 2.1, Dramatic Arc, in *The St. Martin's Guide*, identify which category each of the reading's paragraphs falls into:

   Exposition/Inciting Incident: ________________

   Rising Action: ________________

*Activities for Chapter 2, "Autobiography and Literacy Narratives" (*The St. Martin's Guide,* 13th Edition)
†It might be easiest to continue working with the same reading selection throughout this chapter, but if you choose to work with a new selection for each set of activities, make sure the reading you choose effectively demonstrates the essay's basic features.

Climax: ____________________

Falling Action: ____________________

Conclusion/Reflection: ____________________

2. Using the story you chose as a model, briefly outline an experience or event of your own that you might want to write about for your narrative. Use complete sentences. Try to acknowledge all five stages of the dramatic arc, noting the feature in parenthesis after you have addressed it.

   Example: When I was only about five years old, I was diagnosed with severe asthma (exposition). I had been warned to stop playing if I ran out of breath or started to wheeze, but I kept playing in a really competitive soccer match even though I felt myself getting light-headed (rising action). Just as I stole the ball right in front of the opponent's goal, I passed out (climax). I woke up in the hospital with an IV in my arm and deep pain in my lungs (falling action). That experience made me realize I wasn't invincible and would have to take my asthma seriously (conclusion).

   ____

   ____

   ____

   ____

   ____

   ____

   ____

Testing the Dramatic Potential of Your Story

Make sure your narrative has all of the required elements for a full narrative arc. Use your brief narrative to complete the following statements:

➤ My audience will need to know ____________________ in order to understand my story. (exposition)

➤ I can create tension by describing ____________________. (rising action)

➤ The most critical moment of my story is when ________________. (climax)

➤ After that, ________________ happened. (falling action)

➤ Because of what happened to me, I now realize ________________. (conclusion)

Identifying and Developing an Action Sequence

1. Choose the reading you found most active, or the one your instructor has assigned. Identify a passage in which the author creates an **action sequence** using active verbs that move the story along. (See the discussion of **action sequences** in Chapter 2 of *The St. Martin's Guide* if you need help identifying one.) Write out a sentence from the passage that you find particularly engaging.

____

____

____

2. Explain in a sentence or two what makes the passage engaging. For instance, you might identify the specific verbs and their tenses, or you might discuss the overall *dominant impression* that the sentence creates.

____

____

____

3. Next, identify one of the story elements you constructed in Exercise 2 (likely in the rising action or the climax). Write out an **action sequence** sentence of your own that's modeled on the one you identified above.

____

____

____

Rubric: A Well-Told Story

As you develop your own narrative arc, use this rubric to determine whether you are fulfilling the requirements for a well-told story.

Exceeds expectations	Meets expectations	Needs improvement	Does not meet expectations
The story engages the reader with a compelling narrative. It provides enough exposition to contextualize the experience or events without including extraneous details. The action builds tension effectively and culminates in a dramatic climax. The conflicts are resolved in a satisfying way, and the narrative concludes with a reflection that conveys the story's significance.	The story has an effective narrative. Exposition provides an understanding of experience or events, with few unnecessary details. The action builds enough tension to sustain reader interest and culminates in a recognizable climax. Most conflicts are resolved, and the conclusion (perhaps underdeveloped) highlights the experience or event's significance.	The story's narrative arc is unclear or unengaging. Some expository details are lacking or irrelevant. The action of the story does not sustain reader interest, and the climax is unclear or undeveloped. Some elements of the conflict are left unresolved. The conclusion is abrupt or ineffectively conveys the experience or event's significance.	The narrative arc is confusing or too unfocused to convey a clear progression. There are either no expository details or too much extended irrelevant information is included. The story's action fails to create tension, and the climax is absent or indistinguishable. Important conflicts are left unresolved or unacknowledged. There is no conclusion, or it fails to provide closure or convey the experience or event's significance.

Vivid Description of People and Places

Recognizing and Incorporating Naming, Detailing, and Comparing Strategies

1. Choose the reading with the most vivid descriptive passages, or use the one your instructor has assigned. Identify sentences that highlight the use of naming, detailing and comparing. Review the discussion of each of these strategies under the Vivid Description of People and Places basic feature review in *The Guide's* Chapter 2 or the Naming, Detailing, and Comparing sections of *The Guide's* Chapter 14 where these strategies are described in greater depth. Copy a sentence that represents all of these strategies in the space provided below. Underline the word in each sentence that you think relates most closely to the specific strategy:

   Naming example sentence: ______________________________

   ____

   Detailing example sentence: ______________________________

   ____

   Comparing example sentence: ______________________________

   ____

2. Use your example sentences as models and write your own descriptive sentences for the experience or event, focusing on each of the different strategies. Practice describing different elements of your story, such as the setting or the people.

   Naming sentence: ______________________________

   ____

   Detailing sentence: ______________________________

   ____

   Comparing sentence: ______________________________

   ____

Considering What You Need to Describe and How to Describe It

Review the elements of your narrative that will require the most evocative descriptive details. Determine what you will need to describe and how you will describe those features by filling in the blanks, below.

- A character I will have to describe is ______________.
- When I reflect on that person the first thing I think of is ______________.
- I can best convey that quality by describing ______________.
- The most important location in my story is ______________.
- When I envision that location I most clearly remember ______________.
- I can most clearly depict that location by describing ______________.

Identifying and Modeling Examples of Quoting, Paraphrasing, and Summarizing Dialogue

1. Choose the reading that uses dialogue most effectively, or use the one your instructor has assigned. Identify sentences that quote, paraphrase, and summarize the characters' speech. (Review the discussion of each of these approaches to reporting the speech of characters under the Vivid Description of People and Places basic feature review in Chapter 2 of *The Guide*.) In the spaces below, copy sentences that represent each way dialogue can be incorporated:

   Quoting example sentence: ______________________________

   ____

   Paraphrasing example sentence: ______________________________

   ____

   Summarizing example sentence: ______________________________

   ____

2. Use your example sentences as models and develop your own quotations, paraphrases, and summaries of dialogue for the experience or event you are working on.

   Quoting sentence: ______________________________

   ____

   Paraphrasing sentence: ______________________________

   ____

   Summarizing sentence: ______________________________

   ____

Consider which of these approaches is most appropriate given how dramatic or important the dialogue in your narrative is.

Rubric: A Vivid Description of People and Places

As you describe the characters and locations that are critical to your experience or event, use this rubric to determine whether your descriptions of people and places are vivid.

Exceeds expectations	Meets expectations	Needs improvement	Does not meet expectations
The important people and places are represented vividly. A variety of appropriate descriptive strategies are used, including naming, detailing, and comparing. Relevant dialogue is included in a manner that helps portray the people in the story and their relationships with each other.	The relevant people and places are described in sufficient detail using different descriptive strategies, though not always effectively, or the writer is over-reliant on one strategy. Dialogue is included in the narrative where necessary, and it develops the characters in the story or adds drama.	Description of people and places essential to story is too brief or fails to convey critical details, or the writer relies too heavily on one specific kind of description. Dialogue is limited or does not clearly develop the characters or their relationships with each other.	Critical people and places are not described in sufficient detail, or the descriptions are ineffective, unclear, or confusing. Dialogue is absent or irrelevant, and it does not effectively develop the people in the story or clarify their relationships with one another.

Autobiographical Significance

Identifying the Author's Perspective, and Reflecting on Your Own Experience

1. Choose the reading with the clearest statement of autobiographical significance, or use the one your instructor has assigned. Identify a sentence in which the author recounts feelings at the time of the event, and another where the author reflects on the past experience from his or her present perspective. (Review the discussion of each of these strategies under the Autobiographical Significance

basic feature review of *The Guide*.) Copy a sentence for each of these strategies into the space below. Highlight or underline words that indicate an emotional response or a feeling (such as sadness, excitement, happiness, or terror):

Recounting remembered feelings: ______________________________

____

____

Reflecting on the past from the perspective of the present: ______________

____

____

2. Think about the experience or event you are writing about. The difference between how you perceived the experience or event when it happened and how you understand it now can help establish your narrative's autobiographical significance. Use the sentences you identified above as models, and write out your own recounting and reflecting sentences. Be sure to cover both your past and present perspective on the experience or event you have chosen to write about.

   Recounting remembered feelings: ______________________________

   ____

   ____

   Reflecting on the past from the perspective of the present: ______________

   ____

   ____

Determining a Dominant Impression, and Developing the Significance of Your Experience or Event

1. Look through one of the readings, and select a passage that you felt had the most evocative *dominant impression*. Write out below the sentence(s) that you think most clearly demonstrates the overall emotional context of the story.

   ____

   ____

   ____

2. Explain in your own words what impression the author was trying to achieve and how that helps establish the experience or event's significance.

   ____

   ____

   ____

3. Think about the significance of your own experience or event, and consider what sort of *dominant impression* you want to create. Figure out what kind of narrative and descriptive details you might use to highlight the experience or event's significance by filling in the blanks, below:
   - If I had to describe the way my experience or event makes me feel in one word, that word would be ______________________________.
   - At the climactic moment of my experience or event I realized that I __________ ______________________________.
   - The most important person in my experience or event is ______________.
   - The emotion I most clearly associate with that person is ______________.
   - The most descriptive and evocative location in my story is ______________.
   - When I envision that location I feel ______________.
4. Use your responses to develop a sentence that highlights the dominant impression you wish to impart to your readers. You can choose to focus on an active narrative experience or event or on a descriptive passage but be sure to establish a clear emotional context that reflects your experience or event's significance.

____

____

____

Rubric: Autobiographical Significance

As you draft your narrative, use this rubric to make sure you effectively convey its autobiographical significance.

Exceeds expectations	Meets expectations	Needs improvement	Does not meet expectations
The author announces and shows an emotional response to the experience or event. Narrative and descriptive elements convey an appropriate dominant impression. Reflective comments from both past and present perspective clarify the experience or event's significance.	The writer shows or describes the emotional context of the experience or event. A dominant impression is developed, though it may be applied inconsistently. The author establishes the experience or event's significance and discusses his or her perspective.	The author's emotional response to the experience or event is unclear or is conveyed erratically. The dominant impression is not obvious or is inconsistent. The experience or event's significance is general, vague, or not effectively tied to narrative and descriptive elements. The author's perspective is not fully developed.	The emotional impact of the experience or event is lacking. A dominant impression is not established. The narrative either fails to explain or show the experience or event's significance, or the claimed significance is contradictory or unrelated to the narrative and descriptive elements of the story.

Once you have written a complete draft, review and revise it so that you can turn in the best possible version of your work.

Reviewing, Revising, and Editing Your Draft

Revisit the rubrics for each of the basic features (pp. 30, 32, and 34) to see what you can improve. Be sure to check with your instructor for any other criteria that will be used to assess student writing. Then use the activities below to get ideas for revising your draft.

Evaluating the Draft through Peer Review

Once you have a draft of your essay, your instructor may arrange a peer review session in class, or you might want to get feedback from a tutor at the campus writing center. Customize the Evaluating the Draft peer review guide in Chapter 2 of *The Guide* to your own concerns by asking for specific help with comments and questions like these:

- I'm not sure whether ________________ is working.
- Are my descriptions of people and places in paragraphs ________________ to ________________ vivid and clear?
- Is my narrative's significance clear? What do you think is the significance of the experience or event that I described?
- My biggest concern is ________________.

Gather all your reviewer responses, moving from most critical issues – such as whether the narrative arc of the story is clear, the descriptions of people and places are vivid, and the autobiographical significance of the experience or event is fully conveyed – to more specific issues, like spelling and comma placement. Decide on what you think needs improvement: You make the final decisions about which changes to make and which to ignore. The chart below can help you organize the feedback you've received.

Advice from reviewers	Suggestion accepted?	I don't want to make this change because…
1.	☐ Yes ☐ No	
2.	☐ Yes ☐ No	
3.	☐ Yes ☐ No	
4.	☐ Yes ☐ No	
5.	☐ Yes ☐ No	

Improving the Draft

The Guide to Writing section of Chapter 2 provides suggestions for revising your draft, but there are some additional techniques you might use to envision the changes you need to make:

- **Create a storyboard.** On a sticky note or note card, write your thesis or the main point you want readers to get after reading your story, and put it at the top of your work area. Using separate sticky notes or note cards for each paragraph or section, identify important features such as elements of the narrative arc, descriptive passages, and reflection on the experience or event's significance. Does your organization follow a dramatic arc? Do the parts work together? Is your description lively and your dialogue useful to conveying a vivid story? Does every sentence advance the narrative and clarify the story's point? Add notes to indicate how you will strengthen, change, or delete content based on your reviewers' comments and your own ideas. Take photos of your storyboard, so you'll have a record of what you decide even if you lose your notes.
- **Make an annotated outline.** Outline your story using phrases and sentences. Use your word processing program's editing functions, highlighters, colored pens, or some other method to make your changes clearly visible. Annotate your outline to show the changes you plan to make to the narrative arc, the sequence of actions, the descriptions of key people and places, dialogue, and your story's significance.

Editing the Draft

Choose one of the options below to help you identify a few of the issues your readers frequently commented on:

➤ The two problems that teachers or peer reviewers point out most often in my writing are ________________ and ________________.

➤ I sometimes struggle with ________________.

➤ The problems I most often have in punctuating dialogue include ______________.

Reread your draft, correct any of the errors you've identified, and clear up any other issues you find.

Rubric: Effective Use of Grammar, Syntax, and Mechanics

The rubric below can help you review your essay's grammar, syntax, and mechanics.

Exceeds expectations	Meets expectations	Needs improvement	Does not meet expectations
The essay is comprised of sophisticated and effective sentence structures. The words it uses are appropriate to the context, convey meaning accurately, are at the right level of diction, and effectively contribute to the dominant impression. The essay is free of significant grammatical and mechanical errors and maintains a fluent style that is clear and appropriate to the topic.	Sentences are appropriately complex and avoid significant errors of grammar, usage, and punctuation. Occasional errors (awkwardness, wordiness) remain. Vocabulary is generally accurate and clear, but occasional words may be too casual or affected (voice) or may not contribute to the dominant impression (tone).	Several major grammatical errors inhibit the reader's ability to follow or understand portions of the essay, or repeated minor errors demonstrate an inability to observe the conventions of written English. Prose is consistently wordy, and diction or tone is inappropriate. Spelling errors are frequent enough to be a distraction.	The essay displays simplistic or inaccurate word choice, monotonous or fragmented sentence structure, and repeated errors in grammar and usage that cause confusion or even render portions of the essay incomprehensible.

Proofreading the Draft

Proofreading is key to providing your audience with a pleasurable reading experience, but proofreading your own writing can be difficult because you may be too close to the writing to see errors. Whenever possible, set your work aside for a day, or even an hour, and use one or more of the suggestions below to help you proofread effectively:

- Run the spell checker, and carefully consider every suggestion. **Do not automatically accept the suggestions!** Remember that spell checkers cannot identify problems with homonyms (words that sound alike: *too, to, two*), proper nouns (such as *Detroit* or *Jesse*), or incorrect words (*pubic* for *public*, for example), so check the spelling of these words yourself. Create a checklist of words you've misspelled. Use the checklist to identify and correct words that give you trouble.
- Read your essay aloud slowly. Note and correct any issues that you find. Pay attention to sentences you stumble over; stumbling may be a clue that the sentence is problematic.
- Read your essay from end to beginning, starting with the final sentence and then moving backwards to the sentence just before it. Look for repeated words and similar mistakes that are easy to miss in work that is very familiar.

When your essay is as error free and professional as you can make it, submit it.

5

Writing Profiles*

Profiles share four basic features:

- They present specific information about the subject.
- They are clearly and logically organized.
- They account for the writer's role (as a spectator or participant-observer) in relation to the subject.
- They take a perspective on the profile subject.

The readings in Chapter 3 of *The St. Martin's Guide to Writing* provide effective examples that you can refer to as you reflect on and write your own profile. Activities in Chapter 3 of *The Guide* can give you a jumping-off point for your own writing. The activities below provide extra support for reading the profiles as a writer, applying what you learn to your own draft, and revising your draft to create an effective profile.

Note: Writing profiles requires field research – going out into the world to observe the subject you are profiling – and perhaps some library research, too. Conduct this research before you start drafting. (*The Guide* offers useful suggestions for planning and conducting interviews and observations in Chapters 3 and 17.)

Specific Information about the Subject

Recognizing and Incorporating Naming, Detailing, and Comparing Strategies.

1. Choose the reading with the most vivid descriptive passages or use the one your instructor has assigned.† Identify sentences that highlight the use of naming, detailing, and comparing. (Review the examples of each of these strategies in

*Activities for Chapter 3, "Writing Profiles" (*The St. Martin's Guide,* 13th Edition)

†It might be easiest to continue working with the same reading selection throughout this chapter, but if you choose to work with a new selection for each set of activities, make sure the reading you choose effectively demonstrates the profile's basic features.

Chapter 3 or Chapter 14 of *The Guide*, where these strategies are described in greater depth.) Copy a sentence that represents each of these strategies in the space provided below. Underline the word of the sentence that you think relates most closely to the specific strategy:

Naming example sentence: ______________________________

____

Detailing example sentence: ______________________________

____

Comparing example sentence: ______________________________

____

2. Once you have observed your profile subject, review the example sentences above and write your own sentences describing your subject. Depict different features, such as the physical location or one or more of the people you encountered.

Naming sentence: ______________________________

____

Detailing sentence: ______________________________

____

Comparing sentence: ______________________________

____

Developing Topics for Your Profile

Once you have made a detailed observation of your subject, try organizing the information you have discovered by topics. Completing the templates below can help, but remember that you may need to substitute your own categories for those included here:

➤ I could divide up the place I visited into the following specific locations: ______________, ______________, and ______________.

➤ The key people I encountered were ______________, ______________, and ______________.

➤ The most important things I observed when visiting my subject were ______________, ______________, and ______________.

- The most important/evocative/compelling location I observed was ________________________.
- The most intriguing/odd/mysterious person I met was ________________________.
- The most important/exciting/horrifying thing I discovered was ________________ ________________________.

Identify and Model Examples of Quoting, Paraphrasing, and Summarizing Information

1. Choose the reading that most effectively uses quotations, paraphrases, and summaries obtained through interviews, or use the one your instructor has assigned. Copy a sentence below that shows each of the three ways of integrating information obtained during an interview:

   Quoting: ____
   ____

   Paraphrasing: ____
   ____

   Summarizing: ____
   ____

2. Use your example sentences as models and develop your own quotations, paraphrases, and summaries of information you gathered for the profile you are working on.

   Quoting: ____
   ____

   Paraphrasing: ____
   ____

   Summarizing: ____
   ____

Consider which of these approaches is most appropriate given the information you hope to convey. Quotations are most appropriate for well-turned phrases, dramatic facts, or information that reveals character. Paraphrases are appropriate for details, complex concepts, or crucial information that you can convey more effectively in your own words. Summaries are most appropriate for background and less vital information.

Rubric: Specific Information about the Subject

As you draft your profile, use this rubric to determine whether you are providing enough specific information about the subject.

Exceeds expectations	Meets expectations	Needs improvement	Does not meet expectations
Important information about the subject is conveyed with ample detail using a variety of appropriate descriptive strategies, including naming, detailing, and comparing. Relevant information is presented topically and through appropriate use of quotation, paraphrase, and summary where appropriate.	Information about the subject is conveyed with adequate detail using different descriptive strategies. The descriptions are not always effective, or the author relies too much on one strategy. Information is presented topically using quotation, paraphrase, and summary, though content and method of presentation may not always be well matched. (For example, a quotation would have worked better as a summary or paraphrase.)	Information about people and places essential to the profile is too brief or fails to convey critical details, or the writer relies too heavily on one type of description. Information is limited or is not conveyed through effective use of quotation, paraphrase, and summary.	Essential information about people and places is omitted or not included in sufficient detail, or the depictions of the subject are ineffective, unclear, or confusing. Information necessary for understanding the profile subject is incomplete or relies so heavily on one form of presentation (such as quotation) that the profile shows little discernment by the writer.

A Clear, Logical Organization

Examining and Determining an Appropriate Organizational Plan

1. Choose one of the readings from Chapter 3, or another reading your instructor has assigned, that has a clear organizational plan. What cues does the profile use: *narrative*, *spatial*, *topical*, or *logical*? (See the list of cues in Chapter 3 of *The Guide* for examples.) Use the spaces below to write down the cues you find but keep in mind that not every profile will include all cue types:

   Narrative cues: ______________________________

   ____

   Spatial cues: ______________________________

   ____

   Topical or logical cues: ______________________________

   ____

2. Most profiles will use a mix of organizational strategies but will have an overall organizational plan that is either **narrative** (telling a story, much like the dramatic arc from the remembered-event essay), **spatial** (taking the reader on a tour of the location), or **topical** (based on organizing what it presents into related categories). Review the profile you drew examples from and determine which of these organizational strategies you think the essay as a whole relies on.

   ➤ The essay ____________________, written by ____________________, is organized primarily (circle one) **narratively / spatially / topically**.

   In a sentence or two, explain why you think the author chose that plan type:

   ____

   ____

3. Which organizational plan do you think will work best overall for your profile?

   ➤ The overall organization for my profile will be (circle one) **narrative / spatial / topical** because ____

   ____

Organizing and Outlining Your Profile

1. Fill in the blanks below, and then consider how you can most effectively use that plan type to convey the information you have gathered.

   ➤ I can engage my audience by describing [a person or a location, for example] that will help them understand that my profile is really about [how we try to ignore our own conflicts or struggles, for example].

   ➤ I then need to let them know ____________________ so that I can show them that I discovered ____________________.

   ➤ The most surprising thing I discovered was ____________________. I can show this by describing ____________________.

   ➤ I plan to close my profile by focusing on ____________________, where I discovered ____________________.

None of these sentences dictate a specific structure, but they can help you do two things:

- Think about the most effective way to convey what you learned about your subject through observations and interviews.
- Catch and keep your readers' interest.

2. Develop an outline for your profile. Depending on what you find most effective or on what your instructor recommends, you can write a formal topic or sentence outline, a simple scratch outline, or even a cluster diagram. (For details about creating a cluster diagram or an outline see Chapters 11 and 12.)

Rubric: A Clear, Logical Organization

As you draft your profile, use this rubric to determine whether your composition is organized clearly and logically.

Exceeds expectations	Meets expectations	Needs improvement	Does not meet expectations
The profile is generally organized along a plan that is narrative, spatial, or topical as is appropriate to the subject being profiled. Effective cues are given for transitions between sections of the essay.	The profile is organized narratively, spatially, or topically, and this structure is generally effective for the subject being profiled. Appropriate transitions between sections of the essay are used, though they may sometimes be ineffective.	The structural plan of the profile is either unclear or erratic, mixing narrative, spatial, and topical elements in a way that does not convey information effectively. Transitions are missing, ineffective, or formulaic.	The profile lacks a clear organizational plan and information is presented in an illogical or unclear order. Transitions are absent or inappropriate.

The Writer's Role

Identifying the Role the Writer Assumes and Determining Your Own Role in the Profile

1. Identify a sentence in a reading of your choice, or one your instructor has assigned, in which the author clearly indicates his or her role as either a **spectator** (observing but not participating), or a **participant-observer** (actively participating in the what's being profiled). (Review the discussion of each of these strategies in Chapter 3 of *The Guide.*) Write the sentence in the space below:

___

___

___

2. Why do you think the author chose the role of **spectator** or **participant-observer**? Briefly respond to one of the following questions in a sentence or two:
   - How does the choice of subject affect the author's choice of role?
   - How would the profile be affected if the author chose a different role?
   - Does the author ever take on a different role? If so, where?

___

___

___

Rubric: The Writer's Role

As you draft your profile, use this rubric to determine whether you are effectively conveying your role as a writer.

Exceeds expectations	Meets expectations	Needs improvement	Does not meet expectations
The writer's role in the profile (as a spectator or participant-observer) provides insight into the subject and is used consistently. The author uses his or her firsthand experience effectively to convey insights into the subject or to illustrate the subject.	The writer's role in the profile (as a spectator or participant-observer) is consistent and appropriate to the subject. The author conveys firsthand experience where it makes sense to do so (where it allows him or her to reflect on or highlight the experience).	The writer's role (as a spectator or participant-observer) is unclear or inconsistent. The author conveys her or his first-hand experience without obvious reason or omits that perspective where it could provide insight.	The writer's role (as a spectator or participant-observer) is unclear or shifts without reason. Firsthand experience is conveyed illogically or inconsistently or not at all.

A Perspective on the Subject

Taking a Perspective on the Subject That Shows Its Significance

1. Identify a sentence in one of the readings in which the author clearly uses *telling* (explicitly saying what the writer thinks about the subject) and another in which the writer clearly uses *showing* (description and narration that creates a dominant impression to convey what the author feels). (Review the discussion of these strategies in Chapter 3 of *The Guide*.) Write out these sentences below:

   Telling sentence: ______________________________

   Showing sentence: ______________________________

2. Think about why the author chose to *tell* the reader his or her thoughts or feelings in one sentence and why he or she decided to show the reader his or her thoughts or feelings in another. Explain in your own words why you believe the author made these choices.

3. Practice telling and showing by drafting your own sentences. Use the sentences in exercise 1 above (p. 44) as models:

   Telling sentence: ____

   ____

   Showing sentence: ____

   ____

Rubric: A Perspective on the Subject

As you draft your profile, use this rubric to determine whether you are effectively conveying your perspective on your subject.

Exceeds expectations	Meets expectations	Needs improvement	Does not meet expectations
The author conveys an insightful perspective on the subject or its cultural significance, using both showing and telling where appropriate.	The author conveys an effective perspective on the subject, using both showing and telling, although not always effectively.	The author's perspective is either limited or shifts focus. The profile uses either showing or telling predominantly instead of deploying both techniques to greater effect.	A perspective on the subject of the profile is either lacking, seriously deficient, or contradictory. Showing and telling are either not used or are ineffective.

Once you have written a complete draft, review and revise it so that you can turn in the best possible version of your work.

Reviewing, Revising, and Editing Your Draft

Revisit the rubrics for each of the basic features (pp. 41, 43, 44, and 45) to see what you can improve. Be sure to check with your instructor for any other criteria that will be used to assess student writing. Use the activities below to get ideas for revising your draft.

Evaluating the Draft through Peer Review

Once you have a draft of your essay, your instructor may arrange a peer review session in class, or you might want to get feedback from a tutor at the campus writing center. Customize the Evaluating the Draft peer review guide in Chapter 3 of *The Guide* to your own concerns by asking for specific help with comments and questions like these:

➤ I'm not sure whether ______________________ is working.

- Is my perspective on my profile subject clear and compelling? Why or why not?
- Is my profile subject's significance clear? What do you think the significance of my profile subject is? ______________________________
- My biggest concern is ____________________.

Gather all your reviewer responses, moving from most critical issues – such as whether sufficient specific information about the subject is provided, the writer's role (as spectator or participant-observer) is clear, the perspective on the subject is effectively conveyed, and the composition overall is well organized – to more specific issues (like spelling and comma placement). Decide on what you think needs improvement: You make the final decisions about which changes to make and which to ignore. The chart below can help you organize the feedback you've received.

Advice from reviewers	Suggestion accepted?	I don't want to make this change because . . .
1.	❑ Yes ❑ No	
2.	❑ Yes ❑ No	
3.	❑ Yes ❑ No	
4.	❑ Yes ❑ No	
5.	❑ Yes ❑ No	

Improving the Draft

The Guide to Writing section of Chapter 3 provides suggestions for revising your draft, but there are some additional techniques you might use to envision the changes you need to make:

- **Create a storyboard.** On a sticky note or note card, write your purpose, such as to provide readers with a glimpse into the inner workings of a club or activity, or to present a familiar activity in a surprising way. Put it at the top of your work area. Use your planned organization (narrative, spatial, or topical) to write the information you have gathered on separate sticky notes or note cards and arrange them in groups. Does your organization make sense? Do the parts work together? Do you have enough supporting information for each section? Add notes to indicate how you will strengthen, change, or delete content based on your reviewers' comments and your own ideas. Take photos of the parts of the storyboard, so you'll have a record of what you decide even if you lose your notes.
- **Make an annotated outline.** Outline your profile using phrases and sentences to show its current narrative, spatial, or topical structure. Use your word processing

program's editing functions, highlighters, colored pens, or some other method to make your changes clearly visible. Annotate your outline to show the changes you plan to make. Consider the changes you want to make to your thesis, specific information about the subject that you plan to add, additional cues that could help guide the reader, a clearer or more distinct role for yourself as the writer, or a more compelling perspective on your subject.

Editing the Draft

Choose one of the options below to help you identify a few of the issues your readers frequently comment on:

- Two problems teachers or peer reviewers point out most often in my writing are __________________ and __________________.
- I sometimes struggle with __________________.
- Citation issues most often include __________________.

Reread your draft, correct any of the errors you've identified, and clear up any other issues you find.

Rubric: Effective Use of Grammar, Syntax, and Mechanics

The rubric below can help you review your essay's grammar, syntax, and mechanics.

Exceeds expectations	Meets expectations	Needs improvement	Does not meet expectations
The essay uses sophisticated sentence structures effectively. It uses words that are appropriate to the context, convey meaning accurately, are at the right level of diction, and help create an appropriate tone. The essay is free of significant grammatical and mechanical errors and maintains a fluent style that is clear and appropriate to the topic.	Sentences are appropriately complex and avoid significant errors of grammar, usage, and punctuation, although occasional errors (awkwardness, wordiness) remain. Vocabulary is generally accurate and clear, but occasional words may be too casual or affected (voice) or may be out of keeping with the overall tone.	Several major grammatical errors inhibit the reader's ability to follow or understand portions of the essay, or repeated minor errors demonstrate an inability to observe the conventions of written English. Prose is consistently wordy, and diction or tone is inappropriate. Spelling errors are frequent enough to be a distraction.	The essay displays simplistic or inaccurate word choice, monotonous or fragmented sentence structure, and repeated errors in grammar and usage that cause confusion or even render portions of the essay incomprehensible.

Proofreading the Draft

Proofreading is a key to providing your audience with a pleasurable reading experience, but proofreading your own writing can be difficult because you may be too close to the writing to see errors. Whenever possible, set your work aside for a day or even an hour, and use one or more of the suggestions below to help you proofread effectively:

- Run the spell checker, and carefully consider every suggestion. **Do not automatically accept the suggestions!** Remember that spell checkers cannot identify problems with homonyms (words that sound alike: *too*, *to*, *two*), proper nouns (such as *Detroit* or *Jesse*), or incorrect words (*pubic* for *public*, for example), so check the spelling of these words yourself. Create a checklist of words you've misspelled. Use the checklist to identify and correct words that give you trouble.
- Read your essay aloud slowly. Note and correct any issues that you find. Pay attention to sentences you stumble over; stumbling may be a clue that the sentence is problematic.
- Read your essay from end to beginning, starting with the final sentence and then moving backwards to the sentence just before it. Look for repeated words and similar mistakes that are easy to miss in work that is very familiar.

When your essay is as error free and professional as you can make it, submit it.

6

Explaining a Concept*

Concept explanations share four basic features:

- They present focused information about the concept.
- They are clearly and logically organized.
- They use appropriate explanatory strategies (such as definition and comparison) to convey information about the concept.
- They establish their authority by smoothly integrating information from reliable sources.

The readings in Chapter 4 of *The St. Martin's Guide to Writing* provide effective examples that you can refer to as you reflect on and write a concept analysis. Activities in Chapter 4 of *The Guide* can give you a jumping-off point for your own writing. The activities below provide extra help for reading concept explanations as a writer, applying what you learn to your own draft, and revising your draft to create an effective concept explanation.

A Focused Explanation

Identifying a Focus and Constructing a Thesis

1. Choose the reading with the clearest focus, or use the one that your instructor has assigned.† Identify a sentence or two that clearly conveys the main point of the reading selection. This is the *thesis*. (To learn more about identifying and writing a thesis, see Chapters 4 and 13 of *The St. Martin's Guide*.) Write out the thesis you have identified below:

   ____

   ____

   ____

   ____

*Activities for Chapter 4, "Explaining a Concept" (*The St. Martin's Guide*, 13th Edition)

†It might be easiest to continue working with the same reading selection throughout this chapter, but if you choose to work with a new selection for each set of activities, make sure the reading you choose effectively demonstrates the concept explanation's basic features.

2. An effective thesis for a concept explanation should convey the concept's significance. Why should a reader should care about the subject? In other words, the thesis should answer the "So what?" question. In your own words, explain how the thesis you identified shows why a reader should want to learn more about the concept.

____

____

3. Now try writing a thesis statement for the concept you will explain to your readers. Make sure it shows why your readers should want to learn more about the concept you have chosen to explain.

____

____

____

Deciding What to Include and What to Exclude

1. It is impossible to explain everything about a concept, so you will have to decide which information to include and what you can leave out or assume the reader already knows. Choose the reading with the most focused explanation and the least amount of extraneous detail, and complete the following prompts:

   - Before reading the essay, I already knew ____________________ about the concept.
   - The explanation included information about ____________________, which I was already aware of.
   - After reading the explanation I would still like to know more about ____________________ and ____________________.

2. Consider what information your readers will need in order to understand your concept fully, and what information they might already be aware of or not need to know:

   - The most critical thing I want my readers to be aware of about the concept is: ____
   - Most readers will probably already know ____________________ about the concept.

Rubric: A Focused Explanation of the Concept

As you draft your thesis and decide which information you will need to include or exclude, use this rubric to determine whether you have focused your concept explanation effectively.

Exceeds expectations	Meets expectations	Needs improvement	Does not meet expectations
The essay contains a clear and effective thesis that establishes why readers should find the concept interesting, important, or relevant. The explanation includes all necessary information and keeps unnecessary details to a minimum.	The essay's thesis is clear and demonstrates to some degree why readers should find the concept interesting, important, or relevant. The explanation provides most of the information readers would need to understand the concept and omits most unimportant details.	The essay's thesis is unclear, not specific enough, or ineffective at engaging readers' interest or conveying why the topic is significant. Some information provided in the explanation may be unnecessary or repetitive, and some important information has been omitted.	The essay's thesis is confusing or missing. The subject's importance is not conveyed, and the writer fails to engage readers' interest. The explanation focuses on trivial details, is repetitious, or fails to provide critical information about the concept.

A Clear, Logical Organization

Examining and Determining an Appropriate Organizational Plan

1. Choose a reading from Chapter 4, or a reading your instructor has assigned, that has a clear organizational plan. Identify the thesis statement, a forecast of topics to be discussed (not all essays will forecast topics), and a transition or cue that guides readers from one topic to the next. (See Chapter 4 of *The Guide* for examples.) Write the thesis, forecast, and transition or cue below:

   Thesis: ____

   ____

   Forecast: ____

   ____

   Transition/Cue: ____

   ____

2. Now think about the topics you plan to discuss in your concept explanation. Add a forecast to the thesis you drafted above (p. 50), and practice providing transitions or cues that will guide readers from topic to topic:

   Thesis and forecast: ____

   ____

   Cue: ____

   ____

Rubric: A Clear, Logical Organization

As you draft your concept analysis, use this rubric to determine whether your composition is clearly and logically organized.

Exceeds expectations	Meets expectations	Needs improvement	Does not meet expectations
The explanation provides a clear statement of the essay's main point and effectively forecasts the subtopics, providing a useful guide to the essay's structure. Helpful cues guide readers from topic to topic.	The explanation provides a statement of the essay's main point and provides a forecast of subtopics that conveys some sense of the essay's structure. Cues are provided to guide readers, although they may sometimes be awkward or repetitive.	A statement of the essay's main point is included but is unclear. A forecast of subtopics is missing or fails to provide a sense of the essay's structure. Cues are ineffective.	The essay's main point is not apparent. A forecast of subtopics is missing or is not adhered to. Cues are missing or confusing.

Appropriate Explanatory Strategies

Identifying Explanatory Strategies and Determining Which Kinds to Use

1. Skim the reading of your choice, or one your instructor has assigned, to identify the explanatory strategies — *definition, comparison-contrast, example, cause-effect*, or *classification* — the writer uses. (Review the discussion of each of these strategies in Chapter 4 of *The Guide*.) Write the most effective examples of the explanatory strategies you find below. Keep in mind that, while few writers will use all these strategies, most will use one or more:

   Definition: ______________________________

   ____

   Comparison-Contrast: ______________________________

   ____

   Example: ______________________________

   ____

   Cause-Effect: ______________________________

   ____

   Classification: ______________________________

   ____

2. Think about the explanatory strategies you identified above, and in a sentence or two discuss the ones you would most and least like to try out and why:

____

____

____

3. Choose two explanatory strategies and write out topic sentences for paragraphs that will use these strategies in your essay. Remember that a topic sentence announces the topic or main idea of a paragraph; to learn more about writing effective topic sentences, see Chapter 13 in *The Guide*. Record the specific strategy you are using in the parentheses below.

(Strategy: ____________) Example: ____________

____

____

(Strategy: ____________) Example: ____________

____

____

Rubric: Appropriate Explanatory Strategies

Use this rubric to determine whether you are using explanatory strategies that will be effective for your readers.

Exceeds expectations	Meets expectations	Needs improvement	Does not meet expectations
The essay uses a variety of explanatory strategies to illustrate the concept effectively, and the type of strategy used is appropriate to the information conveyed. Paragraphs using these strategies are fully developed with appropriate details.	A variety of explanatory strategies illustrate the concept. These strategies are mostly suitable to the information conveyed, although occasionally more appropriate strategies could have been used or the examples could have been more fully developed.	The essay is overreliant on one or two types of explanatory strategy. These strategies are frequently inappropriate or ineffective in conveying information about the concept, or the paragraphs using these strategies are not fully developed.	No clear explanatory strategies are used or only one kind is used. Strategies have not been matched to the information to be conveyed. The paragraphs using these strategies are inadequately developed and confusing rather than helpful.

Smooth Integration of Sources

Exploring the Library to Find Information about Your Concept

To find information about your concept you will probably need to do library research. Go to the library or use its online catalog and databases to look for relevant books and articles. You may also be able to use reputable websites. (Look for those with *.edu* or *.gov* addresses.) List your responses to the prompts below. **Hint:** Asking a librarian about how to find useful sources will save you time and produce better results.

- Two terms that I will need to define to explain my concept include ____________ and ____________.
- Types of sources that might have information that could help me explain my concept are ____________, ____________, ____________, and ____________.
- Other information I need to support my explanation includes ____________, ____________, and ____________.

Identifying and Incorporating Quotations, Paraphrases, and Summaries

1. Skim the reading of your choice, or one your instructor has assigned, to identify sentences that quote, paraphrase, and summarize information obtained through research. (See Chapters 4 and 19 of *The Guide* for examples.) Choose an example of a quotation, paraphrase, and summary that effectively incorporate source information, and write them below:

   Quoting: ____________

   Paraphrasing: ____________

   Summarizing: ____________

2. Using the example sentences above as models, integrate quotations, paraphrases, and summaries of source information into your own sentences:

   Quoting: ____________

   Paraphrasing: ____________

   Summarizing: ____________

Decide which of these approaches is most appropriate by asking yourself how vital the information is for conveying your concept. Remember that, as a rule, you will quote a passage when the source's language is particularly vivid or technical, or when you want the words of a respected authority to lend support to your point. You are most likely to paraphrase passages when you want to include the details but the language is not especially striking. You are most likely to summarize long passages from which you only need to borrow the main points.

Rubric: Smooth Integration of Sources

As you draft your concept explanation, use this rubric to determine whether you are integrating information from sources effectively.

Exceeds expectations	Meets expectations	Needs improvement	Does not meet expectations
Sufficient credible research is included to explain and illuminate the concept. Research is successfully introduced and skillfully integrated using quotation, paraphrase, and summary where appropriate.	Credible research is used to explain the concept, though more evidence could have been used at times. The research is mostly introduced and integrated effectively. The work uses a mix of quotation, paraphrase, and summary although quotation or paraphrase is sometimes used when paraphrase or summary would be more appropriate.	There is insufficient research to explain the concept fully. The research is not integrated effectively. There is an overreliance on quotation, paraphrase, or summary.	No significant research is included. Any research that is used is not fully integrated into the writer's sentences. Only one method (quotation, paraphrase, or summary) is used.

Once you have written a complete draft, review and revise it so that you can turn in the best possible version of your work.

Reviewing, Revising, and Editing Your Draft

Revisit the rubrics for each of the basic features (pp. 51, 52, 53, and 55) to see what you can improve. Be sure to check with your instructor for any other criteria that will be used to assess student writing. Use the activities below to get ideas for revising your draft.

Evaluating the Draft through Peer Review

Once you have a draft of your essay, your instructor may arrange a peer review session in class, or you might want to get feedback from a tutor at the campus writing center. Customize the Evaluating the Draft peer review guide in Chapter 4 of *The Guide* to your own concerns, by asking for specific help with comments and questions like these:

- I'm not sure whether ______________________ is working.
- Is the significance of my concept explanation clear? Why or why not?

  ____
- What information about my concept do I still need to provide?

  ____
- My biggest concern is ______________________.

Gather all your reviewer responses, moving from most critical issues – such as whether the explanation is well focused, the organization is effective, the explanatory strategies used are appropriate, and the composition overall is well organized – to more specific issues (like spelling and comma placement). Decide on what you think needs improvement: You make the final decisions about which changes to make and which to ignore. The chart below can help you organize the feedback you've received.

Advice from reviewers	Suggestion accepted?		I don't want to make this change because . . .
1.	❑ Yes	❑ No	
2.	❑ Yes	❑ No	
3.	❑ Yes	❑ No	
4.	❑ Yes	❑ No	
5.	❑ Yes	❑ No	

Improving the Draft

The Guide to Writing section of Chapter 4 provides suggestions for revising your draft, but there are some additional techniques you might use to envision the changes you need to make:

- **Create a storyboard.** Write your thesis on a sticky note or note card and put the card at the top of your work area. Using separate sticky notes or note cards for each topic, identify relevant information from sources you will use to explain your concept and strategies you can use to flesh out each topic. Take a step back and examine your plan: Do the parts work together? Does every paragraph help explain the concept and make the reader aware of its importance? Add notes to indicate how you will strengthen, change, or delete content based on your reviewers' comments and your own ideas. Take photos of the parts of the storyboard, so you'll have a record of what you decide even if you lose your notes.
- **Make an annotated outline.** Outline your concept explanation using sentences and phrases, making clear the topics you will use to organize your draft. Use your word processing program's editing functions, highlighters, colored pens, or some other method to make your changes clearly visible. Annotate your outline to show

the changes you plan to make to your thesis and forecast, the order of your topics, the supporting reasons and evidence you plan to use, and your strategies for integrating information from sources.

Editing the Draft

Choose one of the options below to help you identify a few of the issues your readers frequently comment on:

- Two problems that teachers or peer reviewers point out most often in my writing are ____________ and ____________.
- I sometimes struggle with ____________.
- Citation issues most often include ____________.

Reread your draft, correct any of the errors you've identified, and clear up any other issues you find.

Rubric: Effective Use of Grammar, Syntax, and Mechanics

The rubric below can help you review your essay's grammar, syntax, and mechanics.

Exceeds expectations	Meets expectations	Needs improvement	Does not meet expectations
The essay uses sophisticated sentence structures effectively. It uses words that are appropriate to the context, convey meaning accurately, are at the right level of diction, and create an appropriate tone. The essay is free of significant grammatical and mechanical errors and maintains a fluent style that is clear and appropriate to the topic.	Sentences are appropriately complex and avoid significant errors of grammar, usage, and punctuation, although occasional errors (awkwardness, wordiness) remain. Vocabulary is generally accurate and clear, but occasional words may be too casual or affected (voice) or may be out of keeping with the overall tone.	Several major grammatical errors inhibit the reader's ability to follow or understand portions of the essay, or repeated minor errors demonstrate an inability to observe the conventions of written English. Prose is consistently wordy, and diction or tone is inappropriate. Spelling errors are frequent enough to be a distraction.	The essay displays simplistic or inaccurate word choice, monotonous or fragmented sentence structure, and repeated errors in grammar and usage that cause confusion or even render portions of the essay incomprehensible.

Proofreading the Draft

Proofreading is a key to providing your audience with a pleasurable reading experience, but proofreading your own writing can be difficult because you may be too close to the writing to see errors. Whenever possible, set your work aside for a day or even an hour, and use one or more of the suggestions below to help you proofread effectively:

- Run the spell checker and carefully consider every suggestion. **Do not automatically accept the suggestions!** Remember that spell checkers cannot identify problems with homonyms (words that sound alike: *too, to, two*), proper nouns (such as *Detroit* or *Jesse*), or incorrect words (*pubic* for *public*, for example), so check the spelling of these words yourself. Create a checklist of words you've misspelled. Use the checklist to identify and correct words that give you trouble.
- Read your essay aloud slowly. Note and correct any issues that you find. Pay attention to sentences you stumble over; stumbling may be a clue that the sentence is problematic.
- Read your essay from end to beginning, starting with the final sentence and then moving backwards to the sentence just before it. Look for repeated words and similar mistakes that are easy to miss in work that is very familiar.

When your essay is as error free and professional as you can make it, submit it.

7

Analyzing and Synthesizing Opposing Arguments*

Essays that analyze and synthesize opposing arguments share four basic features:

- They provide an informative introduction to the issue.
- They develop a probing analysis of both sides of the argument.
- They contain a fair and comprehensive presentation of the arguments made by both sides.
- They are clearly and logically organized.

The readings in Chapter 5 of *The St. Martin's Guide to Writing* provide effective examples that you can refer to as you reflect on and write an argument analysis. Activities in Chapter 5 of *The Guide* can provide a jumping-off point for your own writing. The activities below provide extra support for reading argument analyses as a writer, applying what you learn to your draft, and revising your draft to create an effective argument analysis.

An Informative Introduction

Understanding and Presenting the Issue

1. Choose the reading that you felt most clearly presented the issue that the arguments focused on (or use one your instructor has assigned),† and in your own words

*Activities for Chapter 5, "Analyzing and Synthesizing Opposing Arguments" (*The St. Martin's Guide*, 13th Edition)
†It might be easiest to continue working with the same reading selection throughout this chapter, but if you choose to work with a new selection for each set of activities, skim it to make sure the reading you choose effectively demonstrates the basic features of argument analyses.

to identify what the issue is (the crux, or essential point of disagreement) and what position each argument takes on the issue. **Hint:** Look for the thesis, or main idea statement, in the argument analysis, where the writer summarizes the conflict.

The issue discussed is: ______________________________

____

______________________________.

One essay argues that: ______________________________

______________________________.

The other essay argues that: ______________________________

______________________________.

2. As you develop your own analysis and synthesis, make sure you can articulate what specific issue is being debated and summarize the positions the opposing arguments take.

EXAMPLE:

Issue to be discussed: Should freedom of speech be absolute (unrestricted) on college campuses?

Article 1: The article by Ulrich Baer argues that freedom of speech on college campuses should not be absolute because the rights of the speaker need to be balanced against those of the groups whose well-being the speaker is potentially undermining.

Article 2: The article by Robby Soave argues that freedom of speech on college campuses should be absolute because we can't trust authorities, like the government, to protect unpopular ideas.

For more information about writing an effective summary see Chapter 19 of *The Guide*.

3. **Issue to be discussed:** ______________________________

____

____

Article 1: On the one hand, the article by ______[author's name]______ argues that ______________________________

______________________________.

Article 2: On the other hand, the article by ______[author's name]______ argues that ____

____.

4. Effective argument analyses also need to make it clear why the issue is important and worthy of a reader's attention. Explain in a sentence or two why readers should care about the issue you have chosen to explore.

____

____

____

Determining How Much Context to Include

1. It is impossible to provide all the context surrounding the controversial topic in your introduction, so you must decide which information to include and which to leave out. Choose the reading that provides the most effective overview of the issue and the least extraneous information, and complete the following prompts:

   ➤ Before reading the introduction, I already knew ______________ about the issue.

   ➤ The introduction included information about ______________, which I was already aware of.

   ➤ After reading the introduction I would still like to know more about ______________ and ______________.

2. Consider what information readers will need in order to understand the issue your argument essays are addressing. What might your readers already be aware of or not need to know?

   ➤ To understand the debate over my issue, readers must know/understand ____.

   ➤ Most readers will probably already know ______________ and ______________ about the issue.

   ➤ I can help my readers understand why they should care about the issue I am analyzing by explaining ______________.

3. In your argument analysis, you will need to introduce the two articles you are examining and provide enough information to establish the trustworthiness of your sources and your own objectivity on the issue. Include some basic identifying information, such as the title of the articles and the names of their authors, and some information that helps establish the authors' credibility. Fill in the blanks in the templates below for each of the opposing arguments you are analyzing:

- For one side of the argument, I will use an article titled "____________________" by the author ____________________, which claims that ____.
- For the other side of the argument, I will use an article titled "____________________" by the author ____________________, which claims that ____.

Rubric: An Informative Introduction

As you draft your argument analysis, use this rubric to determine whether you have provided an informative introduction to the issue and the articles you will be analyzing.

Exceeds expectations	Meets expectations	Needs improvement	Does not meet expectations
The essay contains a clear and effective introduction, providing the context readers need in order to understand the issue and its importance. The sides of the argument are effectively and fairly summarized, and the credibility of both sources is clearly established.	The essay's introduction shows to some extent why the issue is worth discussing and provides enough context so that the issue and positions are clear. The sides are summarized clearly, and some effort has been made to show that the sources used are credible.	The essay's introduction lacks sufficient context to understand the issue fully, and it is ineffective at demonstrating the issue's importance. The competing sides of the issue are not fully explored, and the credibility of the sources is unclear or the sources do not take clearly opposing positions.	The essay's introduction fails to provide context and does not impart the importance of the issue. Summaries of the competing positions are confusing or are not provided. Sources for those positions are lacking or inappropriate (for example, they may take the same position or even fail to address the same issue).

A Probing Analysis

Representing the Opposing Arguments through Quotation, Summary, and Paraphrase

1. Skim the reading of your choice, or one your instructor has assigned, to identify sentences that quote, summarize, and paraphrase information obtained through research. (See Chapter 5 or 19 of *The Guide* for examples.) Choose examples of a quotation, a paraphrase, and a summary that effectively incorporate source information, and write them below. Try to alternate sources from opposing sides of the argument:

   Quotation: ____

   ____

Paraphrase: ______________________________

____

Summary: ______________________________

____

2. Using the examples above as models, integrate quotations, summaries, and paraphrases from your source arguments. Remember to choose the approach that is most appropriate considering the information you hope to convey: Quotations are most appropriate for well-turned phrases or dramatic facts. Paraphrases are most appropriate for complex or detailed information. Summaries are most appropriate for background and less crucial information. Try to alternate between sources from opposing sides of the argument:

   Quotation: ______________________________

   ____

   Paraphrase: ______________________________

   ____

   Summary: ______________________________

   ____

Rubric: A Probing Analysis

As you draft your argument analysis, use the rubric below to determine whether you are integrating information from sources effectively.

Exceeds expectations	Meets expectations	Needs improvement	Does not meet expectations
Sufficient credible information is included to explain and explore both sides of the issue. Information from sources is successfully introduced and skillfully integrated, using quotation, paraphrase, and summary where appropriate.	Credible information is used to develop the opposing positions, though more evidence could have been supplied. Source information is integrated effectively, and a mix of quotation, paraphrase, and summary is used, although one type is sometimes used when another would be more appropriate.	Insufficient information is included to develop opposing sides of the issue fully. The research that is used is not integrated effectively. There is an overreliance on quotation, paraphrase, or summary.	No significant research is included to demonstrate the arguments on both sides of the issue, or only one side is supported. Research is not fully integrated into the writer's sentences. Only one method (quotation, paraphrase, or summary) is used.

A Fair and Comprehensive Presentation

Presenting Opposing Points of View and Avoiding Bias

1. Choose one of the essays in Chapter 5 of *The Guide*, or one your instructor has assigned, and look for examples that compare the positions and arguments of the different sides in the debate. Note how the author introduces these arguments using neutral verbs (such as argues, claims, believes, or holds) to avoid suggesting bias. Write out one sentence from the reading selection that you think is particularly effective at conveying the positions neutrally, and underline or highlight the verbs that introduce the claims of each side:

____

____

2. After you have chosen opposing arguments to analyze, figure out what specific reasons each author offers to support his or her position. This chart has space for three different supporting reasons, though the articles you have chosen may offer more. Try to identify the three most critical points of disagreement for both sides, and if possible connect each of the reasons one argument offers to a similar reason from the opposing article so that the conflicting reasons appear on the same row. An example is provided.

Comparative Analysis Chart: Arguments

Author	**Baer**	**Soave**
Arguments	**Example:** One reason hate speech should be forbidden on college campuses is because it undermines the right of the marginalized (or weak) to be respected as equal citizens.	**Example:** All speech should be protected on college campuses because, while hate speech may hurt the feelings of some people, it doesn't weaken the victims' first-amendment right to free speech.

3. Using the chart you have created, write your own sentences comparing the positions of the arguments you are analyzing. Use the arguments you identified and connected in the chart to help you determine which specific points to compare:

Comparison 1: ____

____

Comparison 2: ____

____

Comparison 3: ____

____

You can use the sentences you have constructed either to introduce the sources you are analyzing or, as topic sentences, to help you organize your analysis, as you will see in the next set of exercises.

Rubric: A Fair and Comprehensive Presentation

As you draft your argument analysis, use this rubric to determine whether you are giving readers a fair and comprehensive presentation of both perspectives on the issue.

Exceeds expectations	Meets expectations	Needs improvement	Does not meet expectations
Both points of view are effectively and clearly explored in a fair and comprehensive manner. The analysis provides an equal attention to both perspectives, avoids making a judgment about the issues, and uses neutral or speculative language.	Both points of view are addressed without clear bias. The analysis gives a roughly equal amount of attention to both perspectives and avoids obvious judgments. Occasionally, language could suggest that the author favors one side or the other.	One point of view on the issue is developed more thoroughly than the other, or they are expressed in a manner that indicates a bias for one side of the debate. More attention is given to one perspective, and the language is inconsistently comprehensive.	One point of view on the issue is significantly more developed than the other and there is clear evidence of bias for one side. A single perspective is given most of the attention or the composition is less of an analysis and more of an argument.

A Clear, Logical Organization

Recognizing and Using Cues and Forecasts

1. Choose a reading from Chapter 5 of *The Guide,* or another reading your instructor has assigned, that makes an effective use of cues. Find examples of cues that signal agreement (such as *both agree that . . .*) and disagreement (such as *although* or *the crux of the conflict is . . .*). (See Chapter 5 of *The Guide* for more examples.) Write sentences from the reading below, and highlight or underline the cues:

   Cue signaling agreement: ____

   ____

   ____

   Cue signaling disagreement: ____

   ____

   ____

2. Using the examples you identified above, as models, construct your own sentences with cues signaling agreement or disagreement:

   Cue signaling agreement: ______________________________

   ____

   ____

   Cue signaling disagreement: ______________________________

   ____

   ____

3. A strong forecasting statement can be helpful for determining which arguments or research to concentrate on and for organizing your thoughts. However, it is always a good idea to review your forecast in light of what you have actually discovered and written about. Using the points of disagreement or agreement that you have identified, and perhaps also referring to the chart for analyzing arguments that you filled in previously (p. 64), construct your own forecast indicating the points of agreement and disagreement your essay will focus on.

   Forecasting statement: ______________________________

   ____

Rubric: A Clear, Logical Organization

As you draft your argument analysis, use this rubric to determine whether you have organized your composition clearly and logically.

Exceeds expectations	Meets expectations	Needs improvement	Does not meet expectations
The analysis contains an effective forecast of the most critical points of agreement and/or disagreement, providing a useful guide to the essay's structure. Helpful cues are provided to identify specific points of agreement and disagreement.	A forecast conveying some sense of the essay's structure is included in the analysis. Cues signaling agreement and disagreement are provided, although they may sometimes be awkward or repetitive.	A statement forecasting the essay's main points of argument is included but is unclear. Cues are present, but unclear and ineffective.	The analysis lacks a forecast or fails to follow one, if provided. Cues are missing or confusing.

Once you have written a complete draft, review and revise it so that you can turn in the best possible version of your work.

Reviewing, Revising, and Editing Your Draft

Revisit the rubrics for each of the basic features (pp. 62, 63, 65, and 66) to see what you can improve. Be sure to check with your instructor for any other criteria that will be used to assess student writing. The rubric below can help you review your essay's grammar, syntax, and mechanics.

Evaluating the Draft through Peer Review

Once you have a draft of your essay, your instructor may arrange a peer review session in class, or you might want to get feedback from a tutor at the campus writing center. Customize the Evaluating the Draft peer review guide in Chapter 5 of *The Guide* to your own concerns, by asking for specific help with comments and questions like these:

- I'm not sure whether ______________________________ is working.
- Is the issue being argued clear and are the sides apparent? Why or why not?
  ____
- What additional arguments or perspectives could I include to avoid bias?
  ____
- My biggest concern is ______________________________.

Gather all your reviewer responses, moving from most critical issues – such as whether your introduction is effective and informative, the analysis of the competing arguments is probing, both sides of the issue are presented fairly, and the composition overall is well organized – to more specific issues (like spelling and comma placement). Decide on what you think needs improvement: You make the final decisions about which changes to make and which to ignore. The chart below can help you organize the feedback you've received.

Advice from reviewers	Suggestion accepted?	I don't want to make this change because . . .
1.	❑ Yes ❑ No	
2.	❑ Yes ❑ No	
3.	❑ Yes ❑ No	
4.	❑ Yes ❑ No	
5.	❑ Yes ❑ No	

Improving the Draft

The Guide to Writing section of Chapter 5 provides suggestions for revising your draft, but there are some additional techniques you might use to envision the changes you need to make:

- **Create a storyboard.** Write your thesis on a sticky note or note card, and put the card at the top of your work area. Using separate sticky notes or note cards for each point of agreement or disagreement, identify relevant information from the arguments you are analyzing (quotations, paraphrases, and summaries) to support your ideas about why these writers have taken different positions on the issue. Now take a step back and examine your plan: Does each opposing argument get about the same amount of attention? Add notes to indicate how you will strengthen, change, or delete content based on your reviewers' comments and your own ideas. Take photos of the parts of the storyboard, so you'll have a record of what you decide even if you lose your notes.
- **Make an annotated outline.** Outline your argument analysis with sentences and phrases, making clear the points of agreement or disagreement that you will use to organize your draft. Use your word processing program's editing functions, highlighters, colored pens, or some other method to make your changes clearly visible. Annotate your outline to show the changes you plan to make to your thesis and forecast, the order of the writers' reasons you will explore, and quotations, paraphrases, and summaries you plan to use to support your analysis.

Editing the Draft

Choose one of the options below to help you identify a few of the issues your readers frequently comment on:

➤ Two problems that teachers or peer reviewers point out most often in my writing are ____________________ and ____________________.

➤ I sometimes struggle with ____________________.

➤ Citation issues most often include ____________________.

Reread your draft, correct any of the errors you've identified, and clear up any other issues you find.

Rubric: Effective Use of Grammar, Syntax, and Mechanics

The rubric below can help you review your essay's grammar, syntax, and mechanics.

Exceeds expectations	Meets expectations	Needs improvement	Does not meet expectations
The essay uses sophisticated sentence structures effectively. It uses words that are appropriate to the context, convey meaning accurately, are at the right level of diction, and help create an appropriate tone. The essay is free of significant grammatical and mechanical errors and maintains a fluent style that is clear and appropriate to the topic.	Sentences are appropriately complex and avoid significant errors of grammar, usage, and punctuation, although occasional errors (awkwardness, wordiness) remain. Vocabulary is generally accurate and clear, but occasional words may be too casual or affected (voice) or may be out of keeping with the overall tone.	Several major grammatical errors inhibit the reader's ability to follow or understand portions of the essay, or repeated minor errors demonstrate an inability to observe the conventions of written English. Prose is consistently wordy, and diction or tone is inappropriate. Spelling errors are frequent enough to be a distraction.	The essay displays simplistic or inaccurate word choice, monotonous or fragmented sentence structure, and repeated errors in grammar and usage that cause confusion or even render portions of the essay incomprehensible.

Proofreading the Draft

Proofreading is a key to providing your audience with a pleasurable reading experience, but proofreading your own writing can be difficult because you may be too close to the writing to see errors. Whenever possible, set your work aside for a day or even an hour, and use one or more of the suggestions below to help you proofread effectively:

- Run the spell checker and carefully consider every suggestion. **Do not automatically accept the suggestions!** Remember that spell checkers cannot identify problems with homonyms (words that sound alike: *too, to, two*), proper nouns (such as *Detroit* or *Jesse*), or incorrect words (*pubic* for *public*, for example), so check the spelling of these words yourself. Create a checklist of words you've misspelled. Use the checklist to identify and correct words that give you trouble.
- Read your essay aloud slowly. Note and correct any issues that you find. Pay attention to sentences you stumble over; stumbling may be a clue that the sentence is problematic.
- Read your essay from end to beginning, starting with the final sentence and then moving backwards to the sentence just before it. Look for repeated words and similar mistakes that are easy to miss in work that is very familiar.

When your essay is as error free and professional as you can make it, submit it.

8

Arguing a Position*

Effective position arguments share four basic features:

- They address a controversial issue that is focused enough to be presented clearly and fully.
- They take a clear position on the issue and support the position with reasons and evidence.
- They offer an effective response to opposing views.
- They are clearly written and logically organized.

The readings in Chapter 6 of *The St. Martin's Guide to Writing* provide effective examples that you can refer to as you reflect on and write a position argument. Activities in Chapter 6 of *The Guide* can give you a jumping-off point for your own writing. The activities below provide extra help for reading the arguments as a writer, applying what you learn to your draft, and revising your draft to create a powerful position argument.

A Focused, Well-Presented Issue

Identifying and Framing the Issue

1. Choose the reading that presents the issue most effectively, or use one your instructor has assigned.† Highlight or underline passages in which the author identifies the issue and his or her position on it. Pay particular attention to the title and first few paragraphs, and look for sentences like these:

   ➤ Some people say ______________________, but I say ______________________ because ______________________.

   ➤ Many people argue that ______________________, but I think they're mistaken because ______________________.

*Activities for Chapter 6, "Arguing a Position" (*The St. Martin's Guide*, 13th Edition)

†It might be easiest to continue working with the same reading selection throughout this chapter, but if you choose to work with a new selection for each set of activities, make sure the reading you choose effectively demonstrates the basic features of arguments for a position.

2. Using the same reading, note how the author frames the issue by pointing out why the issue is important or significant, who benefits and who suffers, or what values are at stake. Using quotation or paraphrase, indicate in a sentence or two how the author frames the issue for readers.

 ____

 ____

3. A position argument makes a logical, persuasive claim about a controversial issue (one about which people can reasonably disagree). To identify arguable claims that can serve as the starting point for your own argument essay, try completing one or more of these prompts:

   ➤ I recently had a heated discussion with [a friend/an acquaintance/a family member] about __________ because [she/he] believes __________ and I believe __________.

   ➤ I'm worried about __________, and I hope people will realize we need to __________.

   ➤ Our [community/campus] would be a better place if we were able to __________ because __________.

4. Once you've identified one or more controversial issues you might be interested in taking a position on, try identifying what people support or oppose.

   Example: "Some people believe professors should including trigger warnings in their syllabi to prepare students who may confront distressing topics, but other people believe they should not be required to because it restricts or limits topics available for academic scrutiny."

 ____

 ____

 ____

Identifying the Audience and Purpose for Your Argument Essay

Figuring out what your audience already knows and does not know about the topic is crucial to writing a persuasive argument. It is also critical to consider your purpose in addressing that audience and how you can engage readers who might be skeptical of or even disagree with your position. If you consider what they already believe or know, you will be able to determine what you need to prove and what kinds of evidence will be most convincing. It will also be vital to reflect on how your audience's opinions and attitudes may differ from your own. What are you trying to achieve by writing to them? Complete the following prompts to analyze your audience.

➤ My readers will probably already know __________.

➤ One thing most people don't know about the issue is __________.

- Readers who might disagree with my position are likely to believe ____________________.

- I may convince those who do not agree with my perspective to take my argument seriously if ____________________.

- The kind of evidence that this audience will find convincing is most likely ____________________.

- My purpose for writing is ____________________.

Rubric: A Focused, Well-Presented Issue

As you draft your position argument, use this rubric to determine whether your issue is clearly focused and engagingly presented.

Exceeds expectations	Meets expectations	Needs improvement	Does not meet expectations
The issue is controversial, arguable, and compelling. The introduction conveys the issue's significance, provides any context readers might need, and does so in a clear and engaging way. The issue is framed in a way that encourages an open-minded debate.	The issue is controversial but may be a bit too broad or awkwardly focused. The introduction provides most of the context readers need to understand the issue and its significance.	The issue selected is too general, too specific, or too one-sided. The introduction doesn't engage readers and doesn't provide enough context for readers to understand the issue and its significance.	The issue is unclear, uncontroversial, or focused on a readily resolved factual matter. The introduction fails to provide necessary background information or make the significance of the issue clear.

A Well-Supported Position

Identifying and Drafting a Thesis

1. Choose the most convincing reading, or use a reading your instructor has assigned. Paraphrase the author's thesis. (Make sure you use your own words and sentence patterns.) By doing so, you will internalize your understanding of the author's position and will be more likely to remember it and understand how it affects the rest of the essay.

____

____

____

2. Next, list the main reasons the author uses to support her or his position. **Hint:** Look for the topic sentences, the sentence in the paragraph that all the other sentences explain or discuss. The topic sentence is likely to be the most general in the paragraph or set of paragraphs.

____

____

____

3. Finally, list the kinds of evidence the writer uses to support her or his position. **Hint:** Look for quotations or paraphrases of comments from experts, as well as facts and statistics, examples, comparisons, definitions, causes or effects, and so on.

____

____

____

4. Now try drafting a tentative claim of your own, stating your position on a controversial issue. You could adapt the structure of the thesis statement you paraphrased above (p. 72), or you could simply state what you are for or against.

   Example: "I think it's great if professors include trigger warnings in their syllabi for sensitive topics if they want to, but I'm against requiring them to do so."

____

____

____

5. To make a persuasive case for your position, you may need to qualify your claim (using words like *probably*, *perhaps*, *in X circumstances*, and so on) to ensure you don't make a stronger claim than you can defend.

   ➤ If I had to qualify my position, I would limit it by including/excluding:
   ____

   ____.

Using Logos, Ethos, and Pathos to Develop Convincing Support

Effective arguments use different strategies, or *appeals*, to convince readers to accept (or at least seriously consider) the writer's position. They may appeal to readers' reason and logic (logos), their respect for the writer's credibility and fairness (ethos), or their emotions and values (pathos). How can you use appeals to logos, ethos, and pathos to strengthen your position argument?

- I can appeal to logos by using these facts or statistics:
  ____
- I can appeal to ethos by quoting these well-respected sources:
  ____
- I can appeal to pathos by relating this story that demonstrates shared values:
  ____

Exploring the Library to Find Background Information and Supporting Evidence

To find information about the issue you are analyzing, you will probably need to do library research. Go to the library or use its online catalog and databases to look for relevant books and articles. You may also be able to use online sources from reputable websites. (Look for those with *.edu* or *.gov* addresses.) Asking a librarian how to find useful sources will save you time and may produce better results. Once you have found a promising source, annotate it to identify potential quotes or arguments that you can paraphrase or summarize. You can also create an annotated working bibliography (described in Chapter 17 of *The Guide*). Answering the questions and filing in the blanks in the prompts below can help you determine how to develop such annotations. You can repeat this exercise for multiple sources.

- I plan to use the article ____________ by ____________ to make the argument that ____________.
- The most significant quote that I can use from the article is ____________
  ____________.
- I can follow up this quote by noting that it proves or demonstrates ____________
  ____________.

Rubric: A Well-Supported Position

As you draft your position argument, use this rubric to make sure you clearly assert and support your position, provide enough relevant and reliable evidence, and integrate that evidence skillfully into your paragraphs.

Exceeds expectations	Meets expectations	Needs improvement	Does not meet expectations
The thesis effectively asserts the author's position and appropriately qualifies the claim. Sufficient credible evidence is included that relates clearly to the thesis and furthers the author's argument. That evidence is successfully introduced and skillfully integrated into paragraphs. A variety of evidence is presented that appeals to readers' reason (logos), values (ethos), and emotions (pathos). The meaning of the evidence is clearly explained. Sources are properly cited.	The thesis clearly states the author's position and makes an appropriate claim. Sufficient evidence is provided to support the author's thesis, but it may not always be well integrated into the essay. Claims are well-supported in paragraphs, although paragraphs may not always focus on a single topic. There is some variety of evidence, including appeals to logos, ethos, or pathos, and evidence is explained. Sources are cited, though with some stylistic errors.	The thesis doesn't clearly state the position or may be too broad or unqualified. There is evidence, but it is ineffective or lacks credibility, or is not always relevant to the author's point. The evidence may not be clearly introduced or integrated into topical paragraphs. Evidence is of a limited variety or may make only one type of appeal (ethos, logos, or pathos) and is not explained. Sources are uncited or cited incorrectly.	The thesis is unclear or shifts positions, or it is untenable or significantly overstated. Evidence is lacking, is clearly biased, or is irrelevant to (and may even contradict) the author's position. The evidence in not integrated and may not be clearly distinguished from the writer's own ideas. Evidence is of only one kind or is irrelevant and is not explained. Sources are not cited.

An Effective Response to Opposing Views

Identifying Objections and Developing a Response

1. Choose one of the readings from Chapter 6 of *The Guide* or one your instructor has assigned. Consider how the author responds to possible objections. Skim the essay and highlight or underline any objections. **Hint:** Look for cues like "Some say ________," or "Other people might think X, but ________." Pay particular attention to how these objections are connected to the specific reasons the author offers.
2. Identify where and how the author responds to these objections, and make a note of the method(s) he or she uses:
   - Does the author *concede* (accept) the criticism and alter her or his position in response?
     - ➤ X makes a good point when she says ________; she's right to take the needs/thoughts/beliefs of ________ into consideration.

- Does the author *refute* (argue against) the opposing position, offering reasons and evidence that the criticism fails?
  - ➤ X argues that ____________________, but I think they're misinterpreting the evidence. Here's how: ____________________.
- Does the author concede and then refute the criticism (the concession-refutation move)?
  - ➤ Granted, X can be a problem, but we can work around it by doing ____________________, ____________________, or ____________________.

3. Now that you've looked closely at how one author responds to opposing views, try writing a response to someone who disagrees with your position: Point out a potential objection to your argument, and respond to it by conceding, refuting, or using the concession-refutation move.

____

____

____

Finding Opposing Views and Effective Responses

To identify possible opposing views and figure out how to respond, start by playing devil's advocate. Make a three-column chart. List all your best reasons to the left, how an opponent might respond in the middle, and your rebuttal in the right-hand column.

My reasons	Opposing views	My responses

For the third column, you can come up with your own responses or conduct research to see how others have responded to opposing viewpoints.

Exploring Opposing Viewpoints

With your three-column list in hand, get together with a few classmates or a friend to discuss whether the opposing arguments you've come up with have any of the following issues:

- **Credibility:** Is the source an expert? Is there evidence that the source is biased? Are there other reasons to question the accuracy or credibility of the argument?

- **Relevance:** When was the argument made—recently or long ago? Has anything changed significantly since then? Is the argument still valid? Does the argument address the same situation in the same place that you are talking about?
- **Counterexamples:** Can you identify examples, anecdotes, or stories that undermine opposing views?

Rubric: An Effective Response to Opposing Views

As you draft your position argument, use this rubric to determine whether you have identified and responded to the most important opposing views on your issue.

Exceeds expectations	Meets expectations	Needs improvement	Does not meet expectations
Objections and opposing arguments are presented fairly and correspond to likely concerns an audience might have. The author uses a variety of strategies for responding, including refuting flawed opposing views and conceding valid concerns. The opposing views are treated with respect and are addressed without bias.	Objections and opposing arguments are addressed and are relevant (but perhaps not central) to the issue. The author refutes or concedes these concerns appropriately. A reasonable degree of objectivity is maintained, though occasionally the tone may seem a bit shrill or dismissive.	Objections are weak, and the most obvious opposing arguments aren't fully addressed. The author relies entirely on refutation or concedes enough to undermine the thesis. Bias is evident, and significant issues or concerns are inappropriately dismissed. The tone sometimes sounds hostile.	Objections and opposing arguments are missing or irrelevant. The author fails to respond to key objections or does so ineffectively. There is clear evidence of bias or a lack of consideration of alternative perspectives. The tone is hostile to opposing views.

A Clear, Logical Organization

Understanding How an Essay Is Organized and Creating an Outline of Your Own

1. Choose one of the readings from Chapter 6, or another reading your instructor has assigned, and identify the main reasons the author provides in support of the thesis. **Hint:** Look to see if the author *forecasts* the main reasons in or near the thesis. List the author's reasons here:

   ______________________ ______________________

   ______________________ ______________________

2. Most argument essays will be composed of body paragraphs that provide reasons for taking a position and offer supporting evidence. Review your invention writing, and present your reasons in a logical order:

Topic of first body paragraph:

____

Evidence:

____

____

____

Topic of second body paragraph:

____

Evidence:

____

____

____

Continue until you have sketched a plan for all your body paragraphs.

3. Skim the essay, highlighting or circling the transitional words and phrases that connect paragraphs and sentences within paragraphs. Does the author use transitions that introduce:
   - another item in a series: *first, second, next, in addition, similarly*
   - an example: *for instance, specifically, namely*
   - a conclusion or summary: *finally, all in all, of course*
   - a concession: *granted, certainly, to be sure*
   - an opposing view: *yet, on the other hand, however*
4. Now outline your own position argument, using the thesis statement, topic sentences, and supporting reasons and evidence that you developed in the previous activities. Depending on what your instructor recommends, you can write a formal topic or sentence outline, draft a simple scratch outline, or even draw a cluster diagram. (For more about creating an outline, see Chapters 11 and 12; for more about creating a cluster diagram, see Chapter 11.)
5. Using the thesis you have constructed and the outline you developed in the exercise above, write out your own forecasting statement. Indicate the key reasons for the position you hold on the controversial issue you are arguing about.

____

____

____

Rubric: A Clear, Logical Organization

As you draft your position argument, use this rubric to make sure your argument is clearly and logically organized.

Exceeds expectations	Meets expectations	Needs improvement	Does not meet expectations
The thesis is presented appropriately and forecasts (or at least hints at) the reasons and evidence the author supplies. The essay is well organized with one paragraph leading logically to the next. Appropriate transitions are used between paragraphs and sentences.	The thesis is clear and logically placed, though it may not forecast the main supporting reasons effectively. Paragraphs are appropriately sequenced, but transitions between paragraphs could be stronger in places.	The thesis may be presented too early or too late or may not be distinct. Paragraph order seems haphazard. (It is unclear why reasons are presented in the order in which they appear.) Supporting evidence may not be effectively connected to the reasons. Transitions are sometimes missing or inappropriate.	The essay may be disjointed, repetitive, or simply lack any discernible organizational structure. The thesis is indistinct or hard to identify, and the supporting evidence may appear without any sense or order or demarcation by transitions.

Once you have written a complete draft, review and revise it so that you can turn in the best possible version of your work.

Reviewing, Revising, and Editing Your Draft

Revisit the rubrics for each of the basic features (pp. 72, 75, 77, and 79) to see what you can improve. Be sure to check with your instructor for any other criteria that will be used to assess student writing.

Evaluating the Draft through Peer Review

Once you have a draft of your essay, your instructor may arrange a peer review session in class, or you might want to get feedback from a tutor at the campus writing center. Customize the Evaluating the Draft peer review guide in Chapter 6 of *The Guide* to your own concerns by asking for specific help with comments and questions like these:

- I'm not sure whether ______________________ is working.
- Are my position and the reasons for it clear and articulate? Why or why not?

  ____

- ➤ What additional likely objections or counterarguments do I need to address?

  ____

- ➤ My biggest concern is ____.

Gather all your reviewer responses, moving from most critical issues — such as whether the issue is clear and well-focused, the position taken is well supported, opposing views are responded to effectively, and the reasons and evidence are all presented clearly and in a logical order — to more specific issues (like spelling and comma placement). Decide on what you think needs improvement: You make the final decisions about which changes to make and which to ignore. The chart below can help you organize the feedback you've received.

Advice from reviewers	Suggestion accepted?	I don't want to make this change because . . .
1.	❑ Yes ❑ No	
2.	❑ Yes ❑ No	
3.	❑ Yes ❑ No	
4.	❑ Yes ❑ No	
5.	❑ Yes ❑ No	

Improving the Draft

The Guide to Writing section of Chapter 6 provides suggestions for revising your draft, but there are some additional techniques you might use to envision the changes you need to make:

- **Create a storyboard.** Write your thesis on a sticky note or note card and put the card at the top of your work area. On separate cards, identify reasons in favor of your position and relevant information from sources you will use to support your reasons. Now take a step back and examine your plan: Do you offer enough reasons? Is there enough evidence to support your reasons? Does every paragraph help support the argument? Add notes to indicate how you will strengthen, change, or delete content based on your reviewers' comments and your own ideas. Take photos of the parts of the storyboard, so you'll have a record of what you decide even if you lose your notes.
- **Make an annotated outline.** Outline your position argument with sentences and phrases, making clear the reasons and evidence you will offer to support your claim. Use your word processing program's editing functions, highlighters, colored pens, or some other method to make your changes clearly visible. Annotate your outline to show the changes you plan to make to your thesis and forecast, the order of your reasons, the evidence you plan to use, and your strategies for integrating information from sources.

Editing the Draft

Choose one of the options below to help you identify a few of the issues your readers frequently comment on:

- Two problems that teachers or peer reviewers point out most often in my writing are ________________ and ________________.
- I sometimes struggle with ________________.
- Citation issues most often include ________________.

Reread your draft, correct any of the errors you've identified, and clear up any other issues you find.

Rubric: Effective Use of Grammar, Syntax, and Mechanics

The rubric below can help you review your essay's grammar, syntax, and mechanics.

Exceeds expectations	Meets expectations	Needs improvement	Does not meet expectations
The essay uses sophisticated sentence structures effectively. It uses words that are appropriate to the context, convey meaning accurately, are at the right level of diction, and create the appropriate tone. The essay is free of significant grammatical and mechanical errors and maintains a fluent style that is clear and appropriate to the topic.	Sentences are appropriately complex and avoid significant errors of grammar, usage, and punctuation, although occasional errors (awkwardness, wordiness) remain. Vocabulary is generally accurate and clear, but occasional words may be too casual or affected (voice) or may be out of keeping with the overall tone.	Several major grammatical errors inhibit the reader's ability to follow or understand portions of the essay, or repeated minor errors demonstrate an inability to observe the conventions of written English. Prose is consistently wordy, and diction or tone is inappropriate. Spelling errors are frequent enough to be a distraction.	The essay displays simplistic or inaccurate word choice, monotonous or fragmented sentence structure, and repeated errors in grammar and usage that cause confusion or even render portions of the essay incomprehensible.

Proofreading the Draft

Proofreading is key to providing your audience with a pleasurable reading experience, but proofreading your own writing can be difficult because you may be too close to the writing to see errors. Whenever possible, set your work aside for a day or even an hour, and use one or more of the suggestions below to help you proofread effectively:

- Run the spell checker and carefully consider every suggestion. **Do not automatically accept the suggestions!** Remember that spell checkers cannot identify problems with homonyms (words that sound alike: *too, to, two*), proper nouns (such as *Detroit* or *Jesse*), or incorrect words (*pubic* for *public*, for example), so check the spelling of these words yourself. Create a checklist of words you've misspelled. Use the checklist to identify and correct words that give you trouble.
- Read your essay aloud slowly. Note and correct any issues that you find. Pay attention to sentences you stumble over; stumbling may be a clue that the sentence is problematic.
- Read your essay from end to beginning, starting with the final sentence and then moving backwards to the sentence just before it. Look for repeated words and similar mistakes that are easy to miss in work that is very familiar.

When your essay is as error free and professional as you can make it, submit it.

9

Proposing a Solution*

Effective proposals share four basic features:

- They explore a focused, well-defined problem.
- They construct a well-argued solution and support it with reasons and evidence.
- They offer an effective response to objections and alternative solutions.
- They are clearly written and logically organized.

The readings in Chapter 7 of *The St. Martin's Guide to Writing* provide effective examples that you can refer to as you reflect on and write a proposal. Activities in Chapter 7 of *The Guide* can give you a jumping-off point for your own writing. The activities below provide extra help for reading the proposals as a writer, applying what you learn to your draft, and revising your draft to create a convincing proposal.

A Focused, Well-Defined Problem

Defining and Framing the Problem

1. Choose the reading that best identifies a problem that needs solving, or use one your instructor has assigned.† Identify a sentence or two where you feel the author most clearly defines the problem that needs to be solved and rewrite that sentence in your own words in the space below.

____

____

*Activities for Chapter 7, "Proposing a Solution" (*The St. Martin's Guide,* 13th Edition)

†It might be easiest to continue working with the same reading selection throughout this chapter, but if you choose to work with a new selection for each set of activities, make sure the reading you choose effectively demonstrates the basic features of arguments proposing a solution.

2. Think of a problem you or people in your community care about. Fill in the blanks in the prompts below to help you decide on a potential topic.

   - One issue that really bothers me is ____.
   - I've had a significant problem with ________________________ recently.
   - Something that has caused trouble for people I care about is ____.

   Using the sentence you identified in an effective proposal as a model, define one of the problems you have identified:

   ____

   ____

3. Return to the reading you identified previously. Note how the author frames the problem by pointing out why it's serious and who it affects. Look for an example of how the author illustrates the severity of the problem and an example that shows the problem's negative effects.

   Severity of the problem: ________________________

   Negative effects: ________________________

4. Think about the problem you identified and develop your own examples that demonstrate the problem's severity and its negative effects.

   Severity of the problem: ________________________

   Negative effects: ________________________

Rubric: A Focused, Well-Defined Problem

As you draft your proposal, use this rubric to determine whether you have presented the problem and its negative consequences effectively.

Exceeds expectations	Meets expectations	Needs improvement	Does not meet expectations
The problem is clearly defined and effectively framed to help the reader understand who it affects and why it is significant. Interesting examples are provided to illustrate both the existence of the problem and to demonstrate the severity of the issue.	The problem is defined and framed so that a reader can recognize who the problem affects and why it is important. Useful examples are provided that show that the problem is real, though it might not seem especially severe.	The problem is not fully defined or is not framed in a manner that helps the reader understand who the problem affects or why it is important. Examples that demonstrate the existence or significance of the problem are limited or ineffective.	The problem is not defined, and there is no framing of the issue to indicate who it affects or why it is worthy of a reader's attention. It lacks examples that show the significance and effects of problem, or the examples are not relevant.

A Well-Argued Solution

Identifying and Creating a Solution

1. Choose the reading you thought had the most interesting or best considered solution (or use one your instructor has assigned), and summarize that solution in your own words.

   ____

   ____

   ____

2. List the benefits the author describes in that essay. **Hint:** This may be part of a thesis statement or could be developed in a forecasting statement that is near the thesis. There may not be three benefits listed, depending on the essay you choose, but try to find as many as you can.

   Benefit 1: ____

   Benefit 2: ____

   Benefit 3: ____

3. Using the problem you identified that affects you or your community, devise your own solution, and list its benefits.

   Solution: ____

   ____

   Benefit 1: ____

   Benefit 2: ____

   Benefit 3: ____

Implementing and Justifying Solutions

1. In addition to identifying a problem and offering a solution, you also have to show that the solution can be implemented. It must be practical, cost effective, and worth the trouble. Using the same reading you have been working with (or another your instructor assigns), determine the steps that will be required to implement the solution. (Not all proposals will offer a sequence of steps that should be taken.)

   Step 1: ____

   Step 2: ____

   Step 3: ____

   Add as many steps as you need to complete the process.

2. Think about the steps that will be necessary to implement your proposed solution. Write down three potential steps needed to put your solution into practice. If your solution does not proceed in a sequence, you may want to organize implementation from the most to least obvious or from easiest to hardest.

   Step 1: ______________________________

   Step 2: ______________________________

   Step 3: ______________________________

3. Demonstrating that your proposal is worth the effort and expense of implementation is important. Briefly consider the costs or burdens that might be imposed by your solution. Identify at least two potential burdens, such as time, expense, or effort, and briefly explain why your solution is worth this expenditure.

   Burden 1: ______________________________

   Why it is worth it: ______________________________

   Burden 2: ______________________________

   Why it is worth it: ______________________________

Rubric: A Well-Argued Solution

As you draft your proposal, use this rubric to determine whether you have created a persuasive and practical solution to the problem you identified.

Exceeds expectations	Meets expectations	Needs improvement	Does not meet expectations
The solution is clearly stated and convincingly indicates how it will solve (or help solve) the problem. The steps needed to implement the solution are clearly described, and the solution seems not only plausible but worth the time, effort, or expense of implementation.	The solution is clearly stated and seems like a plausible solution to the problem. The steps needed to implement the solution are described, though detail may be lacking. The solution seems plausible, and some consideration of the practicalities of implementing the solution are discussed, though more detail could be added.	There is some form of a solution proposed, but it is unclear that this will solve the problem. Insufficient information is provided to determine whether the solution can be effectively implemented or whether doing so is worth the cost.	No coherent solution to the problem is offered, or the solution does not make sense. How the solution will actually be implemented is unclear, or the solution is clearly implausible or burdensome.

An Effective Response to Objections and Alternative Solutions

Identifying Objections and Developing a Response

1. Choose one of the readings from Chapter 7 of *The Guide* or another reading your instructor has assigned. Consider how that author responds to possible objections to the proposal, its implementation, or its potential cost. Paraphrase the objections, and indicate how the author responds to them. Note in parentheses whether the author refutes, concedes, or uses the concession-refutation move.

   Objection 1: ____

   ____

   (refutes, concedes, or uses the concession-refutation move)

   Objection 2: ____

   ____

   (refutes, concedes, or uses the concession-refutation move)

   Add more objections as needed.

2. Identify objections others may raise in response to your proposal and offer responses to these objections. Below are some sentence templates you can use to sketch your responses.

   ➤ Some might argue that it will be too difficult to implement my solution because __________________, but it should be possible if I take __________________ into consideration.

   ➤ Others might argue that this solution won't really solve the problem because __________________, but I think they're misinterpreting the evidence. Here's how: __________________.

   ➤ It is possible that the problem will not be solved because there is still the issue of __________________, but the seriousness of the problem will still be reduced because of __________________.

Identifying and Responding to Alternative Solutions

1. Choose one of the readings from Chapter 7 of *The Guide* or another reading your instructor has assigned. In a sentence or two, identify one alternative solution the reading addresses and indicate how the author responds to it:

   ____

   ____

   ____

2. Now try to come up with an alternative solution of your own that was not discussed in the essay.

   ____

   ____

   ____

   How do you think the author would respond to your alternative solution? Which would be most persuasive: concession, refutation, or the concession-refutation move?

   ____

   ____

   ____

3. It can be difficult to find alternative solutions to your own proposal, but there are handy tricks to help you come up with possibilities:

   - Consider any solutions you might have thought of initially but discarded as impractical or ineffective.
   - Ask a friend or classmate to suggest possible alternatives.
   - Do some research to discover whether others have proposed a solution that you have not considered.

   Alternative solution 1: ______________________________

   ____

   Alternative solution 2: ______________________________

   ____

   If you do research or get an idea from a friend or classmate, be sure to note the source.

Rubric: An Effective Response to Objections and Alternative Solutions

As you draft your argument, use this rubric to determine whether you have created an effective response to key objections and alternative solutions.

Exceeds expectations	Meets expectations	Needs improvement	Does not meet expectations
Objections to the proposal are presented fairly and seem likely. The author uses a variety of strategies for responding, including refuting, conceding, and using the concession-refutation move. Potentially effective alternative solutions are proposed and their advantages and shortcomings are explored.	Objections to the proposal are addressed and are relevant (but perhaps not central) to the issue. The author refutes or concedes these concerns in an appropriate manner. Possible alternative solutions are addressed, and there is some discussion of their potential and problems, though these alternative solutions could be explored more fully.	Objections are weak, and the most obvious concerns aren't fully addressed. The author may rely entirely on refutation or may concede enough to undermine the proposal. Alternative solutions are either obviously flawed or are not distinguished clearly from the actual proposed solution.	Objections to the proposal are missing or irrelevant. The author fails to respond to key objections or does so ineffectively. There are no alternative solutions presented, or the alternatives are more convincing than the actual proposal.

A Clear, Logical Organization

Understanding How a Proposal Is Organized and Developing Effective Transitions

1. In addition to identifying the problem and coming up with a solution, as part of writing your proposal you need to

   - explain how that solution can be implemented
   - provide reasons and evidence to show that the solution will be effective
   - identify and respond to both possible objections and alternatives

   Choose one of the readings from Chapter 7 or another reading your instructor has assigned, and identify the paragraphs that correspond to the main parts of a proposal.

   - Problem: ____________________
   - Solution: ____________________

- How the proposal will be implemented: ______
- Supporting reasons/evidence: ______
- Objections and response: ______
- Alternative solutions and response: ______

2. Now sketch out your own outline, including all of the parts of an effective proposal.
3. Because an effective proposal has so many component parts, it is important to provide transitions to guide your readers from one section to the next. In the space below, identify the transitions the writer of your model used.

   ______ ______ ______ ______

   ______ ______ ______ ______

4. Now draft some transition sentences of your own. Use some of the transitional words or phrases you found in the reading or select your own. Take a look at Chapter 13 of *The Guide* for more ideas.

   Topic of body paragraph 1: ______

   Transition sentence:

   ______.

   ______.

   ______.

   Topic of body paragraph 2: ______

   Evidence:

   ______.

   ______.

   ______.

   Add sections as needed.

Rubric: A Clear, Logical Organization

As you draft your proposal, use this rubric to determine whether your argument is clearly and logically organized.

Exceeds expectations	Meets expectations	Needs improvement	Does not meet expectations
The opening establishes the importance of the problem and prepares readers for the proposal. The solution is clearly presented and the thesis forecasts (or at least hints at) the reasons and evidence the author supplies. The essay is logically organized, with one paragraph leading logically to the next, and appropriate transitions are used between paragraphs and sentences.	The opening prepares readers for the proposal. The solution is clear and logically placed, though it may not forecast the main supporting reasons effectively. The essay is logically organized but could use stronger transitions in places.	The opening fails to prepare readers for the proposal. The solution may be presented too early or too late or may not be distinct. Paragraph organization is illogical (reasons are presented in an order that is unclear), and supporting evidence may not be effectively connected to the reasons. Transitions are sometimes missing or inappropriate.	The proposal may be disjointed, repetitive, or simply lack any discernible organizational structure. The solution is indistinct or hard to identify, and the supporting evidence may appear in what appears to be a random order, and without transitions.

Once you have written a complete draft, review and revise it so that you can turn in the best possible version of your work.

Reviewing, Revising, and Editing Your Draft

Revisit the rubrics for each of the basic features (pp. 84, 86, 89, and 91) to see what you can improve. Be sure to check with your instructor for any other criteria that will be used to assess student writing.

Evaluating the Draft through Peer Review

Once you have a draft of your essay, your instructor may arrange a peer review session in class, or you might want to get feedback from a tutor at the campus writing center. Customize the Evaluating the Draft peer review guide in Chapter 7 of *The Guide* to your own needs by asking for specific help with comments and questions like:

- I'm not sure whether ______________________ is working.
- Is my proposal clear, reasonable, and practical? Why or why not?

  ____

➤ What additional likely objections or alternative solutions do I still need to address? ______________________________

➤ My biggest concern is ______________________.

Gather all your reviewer responses, moving from most critical issues – such as whether the problem is well defined, the proposed solution is well-argued, the responses to objections and alternative solutions are effective, and the composition overall is well organized – to more specific issues (like spelling and comma placement). Decide on what you think needs improvement: You make the final decisions about which changes to make and which to ignore. The chart below can help you organize the feedback you've received.

Advice from reviewers	Suggestion accepted?		I don't want to make this change because . . .
1.	❑ Yes	❑ No	
2.	❑ Yes	❑ No	
3.	❑ Yes	❑ No	
4.	❑ Yes	❑ No	
5.	❑ Yes	❑ No	

Improving the Draft

The Guide to Writing section of Chapter 7 in *The St. Martin's Guide* provides suggestions for revising your draft, but there are some additional techniques you might use to envision the changes you need to make:

- **Create a storyboard.** Write your solution on a sticky note or note card, and put the card at the top of your work area. Using separate sticky notes or note cards for each step you would need to implement the solution, identify relevant reasons and evidence you will use to support your ideas and responses to objections and alternative solutions. Now take a step back and examine your plan: Do the parts work together? Does every paragraph help explain the proposal and make the reader aware of the importance of fixing the problem? Add notes to indicate how you will strengthen, change, or delete content based on your reviewers' comments and your own ideas. Take photos of the parts of the storyboard, so you'll have a record of what you decide even if you lose your notes.
- **Make an annotated outline.** Outline your proposal with sentences and phrases, making clear the topics you will use to organize your draft. Use your word processing program's editing functions, highlighters, colored pens, or some other method to make your changes clearly visible. Annotate your outline to show the changes you plan to make to your thesis and forecast, the order of your paragraphs, the supporting evidence you plan to use, and your strategies for integrating information from sources.

Editing the Draft

Choose one of the options below to help you identify a few of the issues your readers frequently comment on:

➤ Two problems that teachers or peer reviewers point out most often in my writing are ____________ and ____________.

➤ I sometimes struggle with ____________.

➤ Citation issues most often include ____________.

Reread your draft, correct any of the errors you've identified, and clear up any other issues you find.

Rubric: Effective Use of Grammar, Syntax, and Mechanics

The rubric below can help you review your essay's grammar, syntax, and mechanics.

Exceeds expectations	Meets expectations	Needs improvement	Does not meet expectations
The essay uses sophisticated sentence structures effectively. It uses words that are appropriate to the context, convey meaning accurately, are at the right level of diction, and help create an appropriate tone. The essay is free of significant grammatical and mechanical errors and maintains a fluent style that is clear and appropriate to the topic.	Sentences are appropriately complex and avoid significant errors of grammar, usage, and punctuation, although occasional errors (awkwardness, wordiness) remain. Vocabulary is generally accurate and clear, but occasional words may be too casual or affected (voice) or may be out of keeping with the overall tone.	Several major grammatical errors inhibit the reader's ability to follow or understand portions of the essay, or repeated minor errors demonstrate an inability to observe the conventions of written English. Prose is consistently wordy, and diction or tone is inappropriate. Spelling errors are frequent enough to be a distraction.	The essay displays simplistic or inaccurate word choice, monotonous or fragmented sentence structure, and repeated errors in grammar and usage that cause confusion or even render portions of the essay incomprehensible.

Proofreading the Draft

Proofreading is key to providing your audience with a pleasurable reading experience, but proofreading your own writing can be difficult because you may be too close to the writing to see errors. Whenever possible, set your work aside for a day or even an hour, and use one or more of the suggestions below to help you proofread effectively:

- Run the spell checker and carefully consider every suggestion. **Do not automatically accept the suggestions!** Remember that spell checkers cannot identify problems with homonyms (words that sound alike: *too*, *to*, *two*), proper nouns (such as *Detroit* or *Jesse*), or incorrect words (*pubic* for *public*, for example), so check the spelling of these words yourself. Create a checklist of words you've misspelled. Use the checklist to identify and correct words that give you trouble.
- Read your essay aloud slowly. Note and correct any issues that you find. Pay attention to sentences you stumble over; stumbling may be a clue that the sentence is problematic.
- Read your essay from end to beginning, starting with the final sentence and then moving backwards to the sentence just before it. Look for repeated words and similar mistakes that are easy to miss in work that is very familiar.

When your essay is as error free and professional as you can make it, submit it.

10

Justifying an Evaluation*

Effective evaluations share four basic features:

- They provide appropriate criteria for evaluating a well-presented subject.
- They develop a well-supported judgment about the subject being evaluated.
- They offer an effective response to objections and alternative judgments.
- They are clearly written and logically organized.

The readings in Chapter 8 of *The St. Martin's Guide to Writing* provide effective examples that you can refer to as you reflect on and write an evaluation. Activities in Chapter 8 of *The Guide* can give you a jumping-off point for writing your own evaluation. The activities below provide extra help for reading the evaluations as a writer, applying what you learn to your draft, and revising your draft to create a powerful argument in favor of your evaluation.

A Well-Presented Subject

Describing the Subject and Recognizing the Genre

1. Choose the evaluation that does the best job of presenting its subject, or use one your instructor has assigned.† Identify a sentence or two that clearly describe the subject of the evaluation, and write it in the space below. Highlight or underline

*Activities for Chapter 8, "Justifying an Evaluation" (*The St. Martin's Guide,* 13th Edition)

†It might be easiest to continue working with the same reading selection throughout this chapter, but if you choose to work with a new selection for each set of activities, make sure the reading you choose effectively demonstrates the basic features of arguments justifying an evaluation.

any words that identify the type or genre (and any subgenres) of the subject being evaluated.

____

____

____

2. Think of a potential subject for your own evaluation. Consider what subjects interest you. Can you review your subject objectively and provide an interesting and informative description of it? Fill in the blanks below to decide on a potential topic. If there are multiple terms in parentheses, circle the one that best fits your own subject.
   - I really (loved/hated) (watching/reading/playing/examining/exploring) ____________________ because ____________________.
   - The item I'm evaluating is best described as being part of the genre ____________________ and subgenre ____________________.
   - Some criteria I might use to evaluate my subject are ____________________, ____________________, and ____________________.
3. Write a sentence or two presenting the subject you've selected to a potential audience. Be sure to name the genre and any subgenres that your subject belongs to. **Hint:** The model sentence you chose in activity 1 above is a good place to refer back to.

____

____

____

Rubric: A Well-Presented Subject

As you draft your evaluation, use this rubric to determine whether you have effectively presented the subject to your readers.

Exceeds expectations	Meets expectations	Needs improvement	Does not meet expectations
The evaluation's subject is clearly identified and put in context without giving away too much or spoiling any plots or surprises. The specific genre and subgenre are identified.	The evaluation's subject is identified as a member of a specific genre, and relevant context is provided without too many irrelevant details. The genre is identified, though the subgenre may be omitted.	The evaluation's subject is minimally identified, and some context is provided, along with much irrelevant detail. The subject's genre is only vaguely described, and subgenres are unnamed.	The evaluation's subject is unclear, and little to no context is provided. No genre or subgenre is identified, or the genre is incorrectly identified.

A Well-Supported Judgment

Identifying and Constructing a Thesis Statement

1. Choose the reading with the clearest thesis statement, or use the one your instructor has assigned. Write the thesis statement below. Highlight or underline any words that indicate the author's judgment of the subject.

   ____

   ____

   ____

2. Identify the criteria on which the author bases her or his evaluation. **Hint:** The criteria may be included in the thesis statement, or they could appear in a forecasting statement near the thesis. There may be fewer or more than three criteria listed; find as many as you can.

   Criterion 1: ______________________________________

   Criterion 2: ______________________________________

   Criterion 3: ______________________________________

3. Use the prompts below to draft a preliminary evaluation of your subject. The words in parentheses are hints – use one or come up with your own word.

   ➤ My subject is ______________ (thrilling/dull/uneven), and anyone who plans to (watch/read/play/use/explore) it should know ______________.

   ➤ Although my overall evaluation of ______________ is ______________ (positive/negative) my evaluation is moderated by the fact that ______________.

4. Now remind yourself of the genre and subgenre in which your subject belongs, and then list your criteria for evaluation. (You may use more or fewer than three criteria.)

   Genre and subgenre: ______________________________________

   Criterion 1: ______________________________________

   Criterion 2: ______________________________________

   Criterion 3: ______________________________________

5. Draft a thesis statement for your evaluation using the thesis from the reading selection as a model. (See activity 1, p. 97.) Make sure your thesis statement includes a clear judgment and forecasts the criteria you will use to justify your evaluation.

____

____

____

Supporting an Evaluation

1. Choose the reading that best supports its evaluation, or use one your instructor has assigned. Identify an example taken from the source itself—a quotation, paraphrase, summary, or even a film still or screenshot—that illustrates one of the author's criteria. Highlight or underline any terms that make the author's judgment clear (terms like *good, smart, interesting, boring, unimaginative*, or *confusing*).

____

____

____

2. Using the same evaluation, look for outside sources the author uses to corroborate his or her evaluation. These could be quotations, paraphrases, or summaries from a review or expert, or any other outside resource. **Tip:** Not all professional evaluations will use outside sources. Write out the sentence that makes use of an outside source, highlighting or underlining any words or phrases that indicate the author's judgment.

____

____

____

3. Write sentences of your own, using the sentences you have identified above as models. Include a supporting example from the subject you are evaluating and a quotation, paraphrase, or summary of information from an outside source. After each sentence, note the specific criterion that the sentence supports.

   Example: ______________________________________

   Criterion: ____________________________________

   Source: ______________________________________

Rubric: A Well-Supported Judgment

As you draft your evaluation, use this rubric to make sure you have supported your judgment effectively.

Exceeds expectations	Meets expectations	Needs improvement	Does not meet expectations
An effective thesis clearly indicates the author's overall judgment and forecasts relevant criteria. Sufficient interesting, well-developed, and appropriate examples drawn from the subject, as well as relevant evidence from outside sources, are used to support the judgment.	A thesis indicates the author's overall judgment, and the evaluative criteria are forecast, though the forecast may be awkward or ineffectively integrated. Examples from the subject and evidence from some outside sources are provided, but examples could be better chosen or developed, or more evidence could have been used to support the judgment.	The thesis is hard to identify or does not provide a clear sense of the author's overall judgment, and not all the criteria are forecast. Too few examples are used to justify the evaluation, or the examples are poorly developed, or not all criteria that were forecast are discussed. No outside sources are used.	There is no thesis or it is contradictory or confusing. Evaluative criteria are not forecast, and the criteria that are provided seem inappropriate. Supporting examples are too few, too brief, or unclear.

An Effective Response to Objections and Alternative Judgments

Identifying Objections or Alternative Judgments and Developing a Response

1. Choose the reading that best identifies and responds to objections or alternative judgments, or use one your instructor has assigned. Paraphrase the objections or alternative judgments to which the author responds as well as the author's responses. In the parentheses following each paraphrase note whether the author refutes, concedes, or uses the concession-refutation move.

   Objection/Alternative judgment 1: ______________________________

   ____

   (__________________)

   Objection/Alternative judgment 1: ______________________________

   ____

   (__________________)

2. Use the following prompts to develop your own potential objections, and decide how you will respond to them:

   ➤ The judgment I made that my audience is most likely to object to or disagree with is ______________________________.

➤ Readers may object to my claim that ____________ because ____________, but I think they're misinterpreting ____________. Here's why: ____________.

➤ My readers may still not agree with me, but I can at least give these reasons: ____________.

3. Now that you've identified some possible objections and responses to them, develop a topic sentence that introduces a potential objection; in the parentheses, indicate whether you will respond to it by conceding, refuting, or using the concession-refutation move.

____

____

____

(____________)

4. Coming up with alternative judgments can be challenging, but these handy tricks might help:

   - Consider any specific criteria where your evaluation differed from that of your overall judgment of your subject.
   - Ask a few friends, classmates, or family members for their opinion.
   - Do some research: Look for reviews or critiques that offer an opinion that conflicts with your own.

   Alternative judgment 1: ____________

   ____

   Source: ____________

   Alternative judgment 2: ____________

   ____

   Source: ____________

Rubric: An Effective Response to Objections and Alternative Judgments

As you draft your evaluation, use this rubric to determine whether you have effectively responded to objections and alternative solutions.

Exceeds expectations	Meets expectations	Needs improvement	Does not meet expectations
Objections to the overall evaluation and to the specific criteria are presented fairly and correspond to likely concerns an audience might have. The author uses a variety of strategies for responding, including refuting, conceding, and using the concession-refutation move. Reasonable alternative judgments are proposed, and their advantages and shortcomings are explored.	Objections to the overall evaluation and specific criteria are addressed and are relevant but perhaps not fully developed. The author refutes or concedes these concerns in an appropriate manner. Possible alternative evaluations are addressed, and there is some discussion of their advantages and shortcomings.	Objections to the evaluation are weak, and the most obvious concerns about the overall judgment or specific criteria aren't fully addressed. The author may rely entirely on refutation or may concede enough to undermine the evaluation. Alternative evaluations are either obviously flawed or are not clearly distinguished from the writer's judgment.	Objections to the overall evaluation are missing or irrelevant. The author may fail to respond to key objections or does so ineffectively. There are no alternative evaluations presented, or the alternatives are more convincing than the actual evaluation.

A Clear, Logical Organization

Understanding How an Evaluation Is Organized and Developing Effective Transitions

1. A convincing evaluation introduces the subject, includes a clear thesis that states the overall judgment, develops and supports specific criteria, and identifies and responds to objections and alternative evaluations. Choose the clearest reading, or use one your instructor has assigned. Identify the paragraphs (by number) that:

   Identify the subject: ______________________________

   State the overall evaluation (thesis): ______________________________

   State the criteria: ______________________________

   Support the evaluation (based on criteria): ______________________________

   Respond to objections/alternatives: ______________________________

2. Effective transitions provide crucial links between parts of an evaluation. Identify a place in your evaluation where you have to shift from one part to another (for instance, from your thesis to your criteria or from support for the evaluation to

your response to objections or alternatives. Develop a transitional sentence that will help your readers understand that the proposal has shifted gears. (You may want to review the examples of transitional phrases in Chapter 13 of *The Guide*.)

Section 1 (topic): ____________________

Transition sentence: ____________________

____

____________________.

Section 2 (topic): ____________________

Rubric: A Clear, Logical Organization

As you draft your evaluation, use this rubric to determine whether your argument is clearly and logically organized.

Exceeds expectations	Meets expectations	Needs improvement	Does not meet expectations
The introduction conveys critical information about the subject and prepares readers for the evaluation. The evaluation forecasts (or at least hints at) the criteria of assessment the writer uses, and the supporting paragraphs are logically organized. Transitional words and sentences between paragraphs and sentences are varied and appropriate.	The introduction prepares readers for the evaluation, and the thesis indicates the writer's judgment, though it may not forecast the main supporting criteria effectively. The supporting evidence is logically organized, but stronger transitions or more effective transitions are needed in places.	The introduction does not prepare readers for the evaluation. The thesis may be presented too early or too late, or the judgment may be unclear. Criteria are present but they are unclear or inappropriate. Paragraphs are illogically organized (it's unclear why evidence is presented in the order it is), and transitions are weak or missing.	The introduction does not prepare readers for the evaluation, and the judgment is indistinct or hard to identify. Criteria guiding the judgment are missing altogether or unclear. The argument may be disjointed, repetitive, or simply lack any discernible organizational structure.

Once you have written a complete draft, review and revise it so that you can turn in the best possible version of your work.

Reviewing, Revising, and Editing Your Draft

Revisit the rubrics for each of the basic features (pp. 96, 99, 101, and 102) to see what you can improve. Be sure to check with your instructor for any other criteria that will be used to assess student writing.

Evaluating the Draft through Peer Review

Once you have a draft of your essay, your instructor may arrange a peer review session in class, or you might want to get feedback from a tutor at the campus writing center. Customize the Evaluating the Draft peer review guide in Chapter 8 of *The Guide* to your own concerns by asking for specific help with comments and questions like these:

- ➤ I'm not sure whether ____________________ is working.
- ➤ Is my evaluation clear, and are my criteria fully supported with specific examples? Where might I make my evaluation clearer or provide more evidence?
  ____
- ➤ What additional likely objections or alternative judgments do I still need to address?
  ____
- ➤ My biggest concern is ____________________.

Gather all your reviewer responses, moving from most critical issues — such as whether the subject is well presented, the evaluation is well supported, responses to objections and alternative judgments are effective, and the composition overall is well organized — to more specific issues (like spelling and comma placement). Decide on what you think needs improvement: You make the final decisions about which changes to make and which to ignore. The chart below can help you organize the feedback you've received.

Advice from reviewers	Suggestion accepted?	I don't want to make this change because . . .
1.	❑ Yes ❑ No	
2.	❑ Yes ❑ No	
3.	❑ Yes ❑ No	
4.	❑ Yes ❑ No	
5.	❑ Yes ❑ No	

Improving the Draft

The Guide to Writing section in Chapter 8 of *The St. Martin's Guide* provides suggestions for revising your draft, but there are some additional techniques you might use to envision the changes you need to make:

- **Create a storyboard.** Write your judgment on a sticky note or note card and put the card at the top of your work area. Using separate sticky notes or note cards for each criteria, identify relevant evidence you can use to support your judgment of how well the subject meets each criterion, and think about objections and alternative judgments you might have to respond to. Now take a step back and examine your plan: Do the parts work together? Does every paragraph help explain the evaluation and provide support for that overall judgment? Add notes to indicate how you will strengthen, change, or delete content based on your reviewers' comments and your own ideas. Take photos of the parts of the storyboard, so you'll have a record of what you decide even if you lose your notes.

- **Make an annotated outline.** Outline your evaluation with sentences and phrases, making clear the criteria on which you will base your judgment. State the evidence you will use to support your claim and respond to objections and alternative judgments. Use your word-processing program's editing functions, highlighters, colored pens, or some other method to make your changes clearly visible. Annotate your outline to show the changes you plan to make to your thesis and forecast, the order of your topics, the supporting reasons and evidence you plan to use, and your strategies for integrating information from sources.

Editing the Draft

Choose one of the options below to help you identify a few of the issues your readers frequently comment on:

➤ Two problems that teachers or peer reviewers point out most often in my writing are ____________________ and ____________________.

➤ I sometimes struggle with ____________________.

➤ Citation issues most often include ____________________.

Reread your draft, correct any of the errors you've identified, and clear up any other issues you find.

Rubric: Effective Use of Grammar, Syntax, and Mechanics

The rubric below can help you review your essay's grammar, syntax, and mechanics.

Exceeds expectations	Meets expectations	Needs improvement	Does not meet expectations
The essay uses sophisticated sentence structures effectively. It uses words that are appropriate to the context, convey meaning accurately, are at the right level of diction, and help create an appropriate tone. The essay is free of significant grammatical and mechanical errors and maintains a fluent style that is clear and appropriate to the topic.	Sentences are appropriately complex and avoid significant errors of grammar, usage, and punctuation, although occasional errors (awkwardness, wordiness) remain. Vocabulary is generally accurate and clear, but occasional words may be too casual or affected (voice) or may be out of keeping with the overall tone.	Several major grammatical errors inhibit the reader's ability to follow or understand portions of the essay, or repeated minor errors demonstrate an inability to observe the conventions of written English. Prose is consistently wordy, and diction or tone is inappropriate. Spelling errors are frequent enough to be a distraction.	The essay displays simplistic or inaccurate word choice, monotonous or fragmented sentence structure, and repeated errors in grammar and usage that cause confusion or even render portions of the essay incomprehensible.

Proofreading the Draft

Proofreading is key to providing your audience with a pleasurable reading experience, but proofreading your own writing can be difficult because you may be too close to the writing to see errors. Whenever possible, set your work aside for a day or even an hour, and use one or more of the suggestions below to help you proofread effectively:

- Run the spell checker and carefully consider every suggestion. **Do not automatically accept the suggestions!** Remember that spell checkers cannot identify problems with homonyms (words that sound alike: *too, to, two*), proper nouns (such as *Detroit* or *Jesse*), or incorrect words (*pubic* for *public*, for example), so check the spelling of these words yourself. Create a checklist of words you've misspelled. Use the checklist to identify and correct words that give you trouble.
- Read your essay aloud slowly. Note and correct any issues that you find. Pay attention to sentences you stumble over; stumbling may be a clue that the sentence is problematic.
- Read your essay from end to beginning, starting with the final sentence and then moving backwards to the sentence just before it. Look for repeated words and similar mistakes that are easy to miss in work that is very familiar.

When your essay is as error free and professional as you can make it, submit it.

11

Arguing for Causes or Effects*

Effective arguments for a preferred cause or effect share four basic features:

- They establish the subject and present it in a way that will engage readers and motivate them to read on.
- They develop a plausible, well-supported cause-effect analysis.
- They offer an effective response to objections and alternative causes or effects.
- They are clearly written and logically organized.

The readings in Chapter 9 of *The St. Martin's Guide to Writing* provide effective examples that you can refer to as you reflect on and write a cause or effect argument. Activities in Chapter 9 of *The Guide* can give you a jumping-off point for your own writing. The activities below provide extra help for reading cause or effect arguments as a writer, applying what you learn to your draft, and revising your draft to create a powerful cause or effect argument.

A Well-Presented Subject

Establishing the Cause or Effect

1. Choose the cause or effect argument that you find most compelling, or use one your instructor has assigned.† Identify a sentence or two the writer uses to establish the cause or effect he or she will explore and write it below. Highlight or underline any words that identify the cause or effect and the author's focus on it.

   ____

   ____

*Activities for Chapter 9, "Arguing for Causes or Effects" (*The St. Martin's Guide*, 13th Edition)
†It might be easiest to continue working with the same reading selection throughout this chapter, but if you choose to work with a new selection for each set of activities, make sure the reading you choose effectively demonstrates the basic features of arguments for a preferred cause or effect.

2. Think of a cause or effect to argue for in your own essay. Completing the prompts below might help you come up with a potential cause or effect that you could explore.
   - ➤ I've always wondered why ______________________ happens, and I think it may be because of ______________________.
   - ➤ I've been curious about how ______________________ will affect us in the future; I think it will likely make us ______________________.
3. Choose the cause or effect that you found most compelling from the exercise above. Using the sentence(s) you identified in activity 1 (p. 106) as a model, draft a sentence presenting your preferred cause or effect to readers:

____

____

____

Rubric: A Well-Presented Subject

As you draft your causal argument, use this rubric to determine whether you have presented the cause or effect in a way that establishes its relevance, importance, or interest.

Exceeds expectations	Meets expectations	Needs improvement	Does not meet expectations
The cause or effect is clearly identified and sufficient relevant context is provided to indicate why it is interesting or important.	The cause or effect is identified and some context is provided to establish that it is interesting and important, though some details may be dull or irrelevant.	The cause or effect is only minimally identified, and while there is some context provided, detail is lacking or irrelevant. Little effort has been made to stimulate the reader's curiosity.	The cause or effect to be argued for is unclear, self-evident, or preposterous. Context is lacking, and little to no effort has been made to stimulate the reader's curiosity.

A Well-Supported Cause-Effect Analysis

Identifying and Constructing a Thesis Statement

1. Choose the reading that supports its preferred cause or effect most effectively, or use the one your instructor has assigned. Write its thesis below. The thesis may indicate a number of causes or effects. Highlight or underline the words or phrases that indicate which cause or effect the author thinks is most plausible or compelling.

____

____

____

2. Using the same reading, list the alternative causes or effects the author offers and indicate how plausible (or engaging or amusing) each one is. **Tip:** The alternative causes or effects may appear in the thesis or nearby as a forecasting statement. There may not be three causes or effects listed, but try to find as many as you can.

   Cause or effect 1: ______________________

   Plausibility: ______________________

   Cause or effect 2: ______________________

   Plausibility: ______________________

   Cause or effect 3: ______________________

   Plausibility: ______________________

3. Now identify some alternative causes or effects of your own, and evaluate how plausible you think each of these will be.

   Cause or effect 1: ______________________

   Plausibility: ______________________

   Cause or effect 2: ______________________

   Plausibility: ______________________

   Cause or effect 3: ______________________

   Plausibility: ______________________

4. Using the causes or effects you have identified, develop a forecasting statement of your own. Describe your preferred cause or effect and the relative plausibility and importance of various alternative causes or effects.

   ____

   ____

   ____

Finding Evidence and Support for an Evaluation

1. Choose the reading that supplies the most convincing supporting evidence, or use the one your instructor has assigned. Identify the evidence the author uses to support his or her preferred cause or effect. This evidence might be research studies, expert testimony, statistics, or examples. Write out a sentence or two that includes the piece or evidence, and identify the type of evidence that is being used. Try to identify at least two different types of support in the essay.

   Evidence sentence 1: ______________________

   ____

   Type: ______________________

Evidence sentence 2: ____

____

Type: ____

Using the sentence(s) you wrote out above as models, write a sentence or two of your own to support your preferred cause or effect. After each supporting sentence, indicate the type of evidence you have used.

Evidence sentence 1: ____

____

Type: ____

Evidence sentence 2: ____

____

Type: ____

Rubric: A Well-Supported Cause-Effect Analysis

As you draft your argument, use this rubric to determine whether you have supported your preferred cause or effect effectively.

Exceeds expectations	Meets expectations	Needs improvement	Does not meet expectations
The thesis statement clearly indicates the preferred cause or effect, among a series of compelling alternatives. Well-developed paragraphs offer convincing evidence to support the preferred cause or effect.	A thesis statement indicates the author's preferred cause or effect. Supporting paragraphs offer relevant supporting evidence, although more evidence could have been supplied, or the evidence could have been more convincing.	The thesis is hard to identify or does not provide a clear sense of the author's preferred cause or effect. Insufficient or unconvincing evidence is supplied.	The thesis is missing or so unclear that it is impossible to tell what cause or effect is being argued for. Supporting evidence is absent, false, or so unclear as to be ineffective.

An Effective Response to Objections and Alternative Causes or Effects

Identifying Objections and Developing a Response

1. Choose a reading that effectively responds to objections, or use one your instructor has assigned. Paraphrase both the possible objections or alternative causes or effects and the author's response. Indicate whether the author refutes, concedes, or uses the concession-refutation move.

Objection 1: ____________________

____

(refutes, concedes, or uses the concession-refutation move)

Objection 2: ____________________

____

(refutes, concedes, or uses the concession-refutation move) (Add more objections as needed.)

2. Develop potential objections to your own preferred cause or effect, and consider how best to respond to them by completing the following prompts:

   ➤ My readers are most likely to object to or disagree with my preferred cause or effect because ____________________.

   ➤ The reason for that potential disagreement is ____________________, but I think they're misinterpreting the evidence. Here's why: ____________________.

   ➤ My readers may still not agree with me, but I can at least argue ____________________.

3. Now develop sentences of your own that introduce a potential objection, and indicate how you will respond to it by conceding, refuting, or using the concession-refutation move.

____

____

____

Finding Alternative Causes or Effects and Responding to Them

1. Choose a reading that effectively responds to alternative causes or effects, or use one your instructor has assigned. Paraphrase one alternative cause or effect the author offers, and indicate how he or she responds to it.

____

____

____

2. Come up with an alternative cause or effect of your own that was not discussed in the essay. Write a sentence or two showing how you think the author might respond.

   Alternative cause or effect: ____________________

   Response: ____________________

   ____

Does your response concede, refute, or use the concession-refutation move? (Circle your choice.)

3. Finding alternative causes or effects on your own can be challenging, but these strategies can help:
   - Consider any specific causes or effects you initially dismissed.
   - Ask a friend or a classmate to suggest alternatives.
   - Do some research to discover whether others have proposed a cause or effect that you have not considered.

   If you do research or get an idea from a friend or classmate, be sure to note your source.

   Alternative solution 1: ______________________________

   ____

   Alternative solution 2: ______________________________

   ____

Rubric: An Effective Response to Objections and Alternative Causes or Effects

As you draft your argument, use this rubric to determine whether you have created an effective response to key objections and alternative causes or effects.

Exceeds expectations	Meets expectations	Needs improvement	Does not meet expectations
The writer identifies and responds fairly to the most likely objections and alternatives, using a variety of strategies, including refuting, conceding, and making the concession-refutation move.	The writer identifies and responds fairly to some of the most likely objections and alternatives, but responses are not all fully developed. The writer may rely too heavily on one response strategy—refuting, conceding, or making the concession-refutation move—rather than using all three as appropriate.	The writer ignores obvious objections and alternatives and instead responds to unlikely or implausible ones, or alternatives are not distinguished clearly from the writer's preferred cause or effect. The writer relies entirely on refutation or concedes enough to undermine the proposal.	The writer fails to respond to objections and alternatives, or the objections or alternatives he or she does respond to are absurd or irrelevant, or the alternatives are more convincing than the actual preferred cause or effect.

A Clear, Logical Organization

Understanding How a Cause or Effect Argument Is Organized and Developing Effective Transitions

1. A convincing argument for a preferred cause or effect introduces and forecasts the cause or effect, supports the preferred cause or effect with evidence, and identifies

and responds to both possible objections and alternative causes or effects. Choose a reading that seems particularly clear, or use one your instructor has assigned. Identify the paragraphs (by number) that do the following:

Identify the preferred cause or effect: ___________________________

Forecast alternative causes or effects: ___________________________

Support the preferred cause or effect: ___________________________

Respond to objections/alternatives: ___________________________

2. Effective transitions provide crucial links between parts of an argument for a preferred cause or effect. Identify where in your cause or effect argument you have to shift from one part to another. For instance, where you transition from one supporting reason to another or from your own supporting reasons to objections or alternatives. Develop a transitional sentence that will help your readers understand that the proposal has shifted gears. You may want to review the examples of transitional phrases in Chapter 13 of *The Guide*.

Section 1 (topic): ___________________________

Transition sentence: ___________________________

____

___________________________.

Section 2 (topic): ___________________________

Rubric: A Clear, Logical Organization

As you draft the argument for your preferred cause or effect, use this rubric to determine whether your argument is clearly and logically organized.

Exceeds expectations	**Meets expectations**	**Needs improvement**	**Does not meet expectations**
The introduction conveys critical background and prepares readers for the preferred cause or effect. The thesis clearly states the preferred cause or effect and forecasts the reasons it is preferred. The argument is logically organized, with appropriate transitions between paragraphs and sentences.	The introduction prepares readers for the preferred cause or effect, the thesis clearly indicates the preferred cause or effect, and it forecasts the main reasons for the choice, but the order in which the reasons are presented may be illogical, or the essay could use stronger transitions in places.	The introduction does not prepare readers for the preferred cause or effect. The thesis is unclear, and the reasons for preferring one cause or effect over another may be weak or unpersuasive. Paragraphs are illogically organized (it's unclear why evidence is presented in the order it is), and transitions are weak or sometimes missing.	The introduction does not prepare readers for the preferred cause or effect. The thesis stating the preferred cause or effect may be indistinct or hard to identify. The reasons supporting the choice of cause or effect are not forecast. The argument may be disjointed, repetitive, or may simply lack any discernible organizational structure.

Once you have written a complete draft, review and revise it so that you can turn in the best possible version of your work.

Reviewing, Revising, and Editing Your Draft

Revisit the rubrics for each of the basic features (pp. 107, 109, 111, and 112) to see what you can improve. Be sure to check with your instructor for any other criteria that will be used to assess student writing.

Evaluating the Draft through Peer Review

Customize the Evaluating the Draft peer review guide in Chapter 9 of *The Guide* to your own concerns by asking for specific help with comments and questions like these:

- I'm not sure whether ______________________ is working.
- Are my causes and effects plausible and well supported? Why or why not? ______________________
- What additional likely objections or alternative causes or effects do I still need to address? ______________________
- My biggest concern is ______________________.

Gather all your reviewer responses, moving from most critical issues – such as whether the subject is well presented, the causes or effects are well supported, the responses to objections and alternative causes or effects are effective, and the composition overall is well organized – to more specific issues (like spelling and comma placement). Decide on what you think needs improvement: You make the final decisions about which changes to make and which to ignore. The chart below can help you organize the feedback you've received.

Advice from reviewers	Suggestion accepted?	I don't want to make this change because . . .
1.	❑ Yes ❑ No	
2.	❑ Yes ❑ No	
3.	❑ Yes ❑ No	
4.	❑ Yes ❑ No	
5.	❑ Yes ❑ No	

Improving the Draft

The Guide to Writing section in Chapter 9 of *The Guide* provides suggestions for revising your draft, but there are some additional techniques you might use to envision the changes you need to make:

- **Create a storyboard.** Write your thesis on a sticky note or note card, and put the card at the top of your work area. Using separate sticky notes or note cards for each reason supporting your choice of cause or effect, identify supporting evidence and respond to objections or alternative causes or effects. Now take a step back and examine your plan: Do the parts work together? Does every paragraph help justify your choice of cause or effect and provide appropriate supporting evidence? Add notes to indicate how you will strengthen, change, or delete content based on your reviewers' comments and your own ideas. Take photos of the parts of the storyboard so you'll have a record of what you decide even if you lose your notes.
- **Make an annotated outline.** Outline the argument for your preferred cause or effect using phrases and sentences, making clear the reasons you will use to justify your choice. Use your word processing program's editing functions, highlighters, colored pens, or some other method to make your changes clearly visible. Annotate your outline to show the changes you plan to make to your thesis and forecast the order of your reasons, the supporting evidence you plan to use, and your strategies for integrating information from sources.

Editing the Draft

Choose one of the options below to help you identify a few of the issues your readers frequently comment on:

➤ Two problems that teachers or peer reviewers point out most often in my writing are ______________________ and ______________________.

➤ I sometimes struggle with ______________________.

➤ Citation issues most often include ______________________.

Reread your draft, correct any of the errors you've identified, and clear up any other issues you find.

Rubric: Effective Use of Grammar, Syntax, and Mechanics

The rubric below can help you review your essay's grammar, syntax, and mechanics.

Exceeds expectations	Meets expectations	Needs improvement	Does not meet expectations
The essay uses sophisticated sentence structures effectively. It uses words that are appropriate to the context, convey meaning accurately, are at the right level of diction, and help create an appropriate tone. The essay is free of significant grammatical and mechanical errors and maintains a fluent style that is clear and appropriate to the topic.	Sentences are appropriately complex and avoid significant errors of grammar, usage, and punctuation, although occasional errors (awkwardness, wordiness) remain. Vocabulary is generally accurate and clear, but occasional words may be too casual or affected (voice) or may be out of keeping with the overall tone.	Several major grammatical errors inhibit the reader's ability to follow or understand portions of the essay, or repeated minor errors demonstrate an inability to observe the conventions of written English. Prose is consistently wordy and diction or tone is inappropriate. Spelling errors are frequent enough to be a distraction.	The essay displays simplistic or inaccurate word choice, monotonous or fragmented sentence structure, and repeated errors in grammar and usage that cause confusion or even render portions of the essay incomprehensible.

Proofreading the Draft

Proofreading is key to providing your audience with a pleasurable reading experience. But proofreading your own writing can be difficult because you may be too close to the writing to see errors. Whenever possible, set your work aside for a day or even an hour, and use one or more of the suggestions below to help you proofread effectively:

- Run the spell checker and carefully consider every suggestion. **Do not automatically accept the suggestions!** Remember that spell checkers cannot identify problems with homonyms (words that sound alike: *too, to, two*), proper nouns (such as *Detroit* or *Jesse*), or incorrect words (*pubic* for *public*, for example), so check the spelling of these words yourself. Create a checklist of words you've misspelled. Use the checklist to identify and correct words that give you trouble.
- Read your essay aloud slowly. Note and correct any issues that you find. Pay attention to sentences you stumble over; stumbling may be a clue that the sentence is problematic.
- Read your essay from end to beginning, starting with the final sentence and then moving backwards to the sentence just before it. Look for repeated words and similar mistakes that are easy to miss in work that is very familiar.

When your essay is as error free and professional as you can make it, submit it.

12

Analyzing Stories*

Convincing story analyses share three basic features:

- They contain a clear, arguable thesis that asserts the author's claim.
- They develop a well-supported argument that provides reasons and evidence.
- They are clearly written and logically organized.

The readings in Chapter 10 of *The St. Martin's Guide to Writing* provide effective examples that you can refer to as you reflect on and write a literary analysis. Activities in Chapter 10 of *The Guide* can give you a jumping-off point for your own writing. The activities below provide extra help for reading literary analyses as a writer, applying what you learn to your draft, and revising your draft to create a powerful analysis of a story or other work of literature.

A Clear, Arguable Thesis

Identifying and Generating a Thesis

Choose the literary analysis that you think has the clearest thesis statement, or use one your instructor has assigned.† Write that essay's thesis below. Highlight or underline any key terms (or synonyms) and ideas being forecast (ideas that will be developed elsewhere in the essay). See Chapter 10 in *The Guide* for more information about using key terms in the thesis and topic sentences.

____

____

____

1. Think of a potential story you might analyze for this assignment. Your instructor might assign you a story, or you may be asked to select one of the stories in the

*Activities for Chapter 10, "Analyzing Stories" (*The St. Martin's Guide*, 13th Edition)

† It might be easiest to continue working with the same reading selection throughout this chapter, but if you choose to work with a new selection for each set of activities, make sure the reading you choose effectively demonstrates the basic features of arguments for a literary analysis.

"Anthology of Short Stories" that follows Chapter 10 in *The Guide*. Consider what kinds of stories interest you, and also think about whether you can find a good way into the story and enough support for your analysis. Fill in the blanks in the prompts below to help you decide on a potential story for your analysis. If there are multiple terms in parentheses, circle the one that best fits your own subject.

- I've really enjoyed the story "________________" because it made me think about ____.
- I enjoy reading (mystery/sci-fi/fantasy/action-adventure/literary) stories because ____.
- A story that I read recently for another class was ________________________.
  One thing it made me consider that I hadn't thought about before was
  ____.

2. Review your responses and choose a story to write about. Draft a working (tentative) thesis statement of your own by using the thesis statement you copied down as a model:

   ____

   ____

   ____

   You will probably revise your working thesis several times as you develop your analysis, but writing out a thesis early on can help focus your reading and research.

Rubric: A Clear, Arguable Thesis

As you draft your analysis, use this rubric to make sure your thesis is clear and arguable.

Exceeds expectations	**Meets expectations**	**Needs improvement**	**Does not meet expectations**
The thesis is arguable (it focuses on a topic about which reasonable readers may disagree). It asserts a claim authoritatively but respectfully. The interpretation it argues for is complex and goes beyond a surface reading. It avoids generalizations, exaggerations, and statements of obvious fact or conclusion.	The thesis is arguable (it focuses on a topic about which reasonable readers may disagree), and it asserts the main claim effectively. The interpretation it argues for goes a bit beyond a simple surface reading. It avoids most generalizations or exaggerations, and it offers more than a statement of fact or an obvious conclusion.	The thesis is unclear or difficult to argue convincingly. The interpretation it offers is obvious or implausible. It relies on some generalizations and exaggerations, or the thesis is a statement of obvious fact or draws a self-evident conclusion.	There is no discernable thesis or the thesis presents a clear misreading of the text. Any claims are provably false or so general or obvious that no real analysis is apparent. There are significant generalizations or gross exaggerations based on little in the story itself.

A Well-Supported Argument

Examining and Developing Reasons, Evidence, and Explanations

1. Choose the reading that supports its argument most convincingly, or use the one your instructor has assigned. Identify the writer's main claim and the reasons the author provides to support that claim. You probably identified the main claim when you found the thesis, but it can be helpful to restate it here. Briefly restate the thesis in your own words, so that you can see how it connects to the supporting reasons that back up that claim.

   The main claim: ______________________________

   Reason 1: ______________________________

   Reason 2: ______________________________

   Reason 3: ______________________________

2. Identify the evidence the author uses to support each reason. This support might be a quotation, paraphrase, or summary from the story itself, or it might be from an outside source. Write out a piece of evidence for each of the reasons you identified above, and circle the type of support it offers.

   Support for reason 1: ______________________________

   ____

   Type: Quotation from story/Paraphrase of story/Summary of story/Outside source

   Support for reason 2: ______________________________

   ____

   Type: Quotation from story/Paraphrase of story/Summary of story/Outside source

   Support for reason 3: ______________________________

   ____

   Type: Quotation from story/Paraphrase of story/Summary of story/Outside source

3. Identify how the author explains his or her supporting evidence and uses it to construct an analysis of the story. **Tip:** In story analyses, authors frequently focus on one or more characters, the setting or plot structure, point of view, themes or symbolism (the figurative or metaphoric meaning of an image or phrase), or language, such as the *connotation* (cultural or emotional associations) of words. The two student writers in Chapter 10 focus mainly on symbolism and language. What specific words or symbols does the writer whose essay you are analyzing focus on? In your own words, explain briefly how the author uses her own ideas with evidence from the story to construct her analysis.

Support for reason 1 – words and/or symbols: ______

______

Analysis: ______

______

Support for reason 2 – words and/or symbols: ______

______

Analysis: ______

______

Support for reason 3 – words and/or symbols: ______

Analysis: ______

______

4. Now return to the story you plan to analyze and the tentative thesis you developed and come up with at least two reasons that support your thesis. Then identify a potential quotation that you could use to support each reason, and analyze it.

Reason 1: ______

______

Supporting quotation: ______

______

Analysis of quotation: ______

______

Reason 2: ______

______

Supporting quotation: ______

______

Analysis of quotation: ______

______

Rubric: A Well-Supported Argument

As you draft your argument, use this rubric to determine whether you have supported your claim effectively.

Exceeds expectations	**Meets expectations**	**Needs improvement**	**Does not meet expectations**
Persuasive reasons are developed that effectively support the author's claim. Significant and convincing evidence from the story is quoted, paraphrased, or summarized to support the reasons, and the author clearly explains and analyzes that evidence.	Practical reasons are developed that support the author's claim. Relevant evidence from the story is quoted, paraphrased, or summarized that supports the reasons, and the author provides some analysis and explanation of that evidence, though the analysis may sometimes be somewhat superficial.	The author's claim is not obvious or is hard to identify. Some reasons are given, but they do not effectively support the claim. Evidence from the story is used only occasionally. The evidence that is provided is either not analyzed or does not demonstrate what the author claims.	The thesis is missing or so unclear that it is hard to tell what the author is arguing. No good reasons are given to support the thesis. Supporting evidence is lacking or irrelevant. The evidence is not analyzed, the analysis is contradictory, or it demonstrates a misunderstanding of the story.

A Clear, Logical Organization

Understanding How a Story Analysis Is Organized and Creating Effective Transitions

1. A convincing argument for an interpretation or analysis of a story offers a clear thesis that forecasts the supporting reasons to be explored, supports those reasons with evidence from the text (and perhaps outside sources), and analyzes and explains the evidence. Choose a story analysis, or use one your instructor has assigned, and identify the paragraphs by number that:

   State the thesis (or main claim): ______________________

   Forecast supporting reasons: ______________________

   Provide supporting evidence for each reason: ______________________

   Analyze/explain the evidence: ______________________

2. Effective transitions provide crucial links between parts of an argument for a story's interpretation. Using the reasons you came up with previously (see p. 119), develop a transitional sentence that will help readers understand that you are moving from one reason to the other. You may want to review the examples of transitional phrases in Chapter 13 of *The Guide*.

   Reason 1: ______________________

   Transition sentence:

   ____

____

____.

Reason 2: ____________________________________

Rubric: A Clear, Logical Organization

As you draft your argument, use this rubric to determine whether your analysis is clearly and logically organized.

Exceeds expectations	Meets expectations	Needs improvement	Does not meet expectations
The introduction conveys a clear thesis that forecasts the reasons to come. The reasons are appropriately supported by evidence from the story and each supporting paragraph moves logically from one topic to the next, with appropriate transitions between paragraphs and sentences. The conclusion successfully knits the essay together and leaves readers with a sense of closure.	The introduction provides a coherent thesis. Supporting reasons are forecast, but the order in which the reasons are presented is unclear, and the essay could use stronger transitions in places. The conclusion draws the essay to a close, but it could be more compelling or emphasize the importance of the analysis more effectively.	The introduction does not prepare readers for the analysis. The thesis is unclear, and the forecast is weak or missing. The reasons may be weak or unpersuasive. Paragraph organization is illogical (why evidence is presented in the order in which it appears is unclear), and that evidence may not clearly support the reasons. Transitions are sometimes missing or inappropriate. The conclusion is weak or missing.	The thesis may be missing, indistinct, or hard to identify. The reasons supporting the thesis are not forecast. The argument may be disjointed, repetitive, or simply lack any discernible organizational structure. An introduction and/or conclusion is missing.

Once you have written a complete draft, review and revise it so that you can turn in the best possible version of your work.

Reviewing, Revising, and Editing Your Draft

Revisit the rubrics for each of the basic features (pp. 117, 120, and 121) to see what you can improve. Be sure to check with your instructor for any other criteria that will be used to assess student writing.

Evaluating the Draft through Peer Review

Customize the Evaluating the Draft peer review guide in Chapter 10 of *The Guide* to your own concerns by asking for specific help with comments and questions like these:

➤ I'm not sure whether ____________________ is working.

➤ Is my thesis clear and reasonable without being obvious or general? Why or why not? ____________________

➤ What additional reasons and evidence could I provide to support my thesis?

____

➤ Do I analyze the evidence, or do I need to make clearer how the evidence supports my reasons?

➤ My biggest concern is ____________________.

Gather all your reviewer responses, moving from most critical issues – such as whether your thesis is clear and arguable, the thesis is well-supported, and the essay is clearly and logically organized – to more specific issues (like spelling and comma placement). Decide on what you think needs improvement: You make the final decisions about which changes to make and which to ignore. The chart below can help you organize the feedback you've received.

Advice from reviewers	Suggestion accepted?	I don't want to make this change because . . .
1.	❑ Yes ❑ No	
2.	❑ Yes ❑ No	
3.	❑ Yes ❑ No	
4.	❑ Yes ❑ No	
5.	❑ Yes ❑ No	

Improving the Draft

The Guide to Writing section in Chapter 10 of *The Guide* provides suggestions for revising your draft, but there are some additional techniques you might use to envision the changes you need to make:

- **Create a storyboard.** Write your thesis on a sticky note or note card, and put the card at the top of your work area. Using separate sticky notes or note cards for each supporting reason, identify relevant information from the story that you will use to support your reasons. Now take a step back and examine your plan: Do the parts work together? Does every paragraph help explain the analysis and provide sufficient supporting evidence? Add notes to indicate how you will strengthen, change, or delete content based on your reviewers' comments and your own ideas. Take photos of the parts of the storyboard, so you'll have a record of what you decide even if you lose your notes.
- **Make an annotated outline.** Outline your story analysis in phrases and sentences, making clear the reasons you will use to organize your draft. Use your

word processing program's editing functions, highlighters, colored pens, or some other method to make your changes clearly visible. Annotate your outline to show the changes you plan to make to your thesis and forecast, the order of your topics, the supporting reasons and evidence you plan to use, and your strategies for integrating information from sources.

Editing the Draft

Choose one of the options below to help you identify a few of the issues your readers frequently comment on:

- Two problems that teachers or peer reviewers point out most often in my writing are ____________________ and ____________________.
- I sometimes struggle with ____.
- Citation issues most often include ____________________________________.

Reread your draft, correct any of the errors you've identified, and clear up any other issues you find.

Rubric: Effective Use of Grammar, Syntax, and Mechanics

The rubric below can help you review your essay's grammar, syntax, and mechanics.

Exceeds expectations	Meets expectations	Needs improvement	Does not meet expectations
The essay uses sophisticated sentence structures effectively. It uses words that are appropriate to the context, convey meaning accurately, are at the right level of diction, and help create an appropriate tone. The essay is free of significant grammatical and mechanical errors and maintains a fluent style that is clear and appropriate to the topic.	Sentences are appropriately complex and avoid significant errors of grammar, usage, and punctuation, although occasional errors (awkwardness, wordiness) remain. Vocabulary is generally accurate and clear, but occasional words may be too casual or affected (voice) or may be out of keeping with the overall tone.	Several major grammatical errors inhibit the reader's ability to follow or understand portions of the essay, or repeated minor errors demonstrate an inability to observe the conventions of written English. Prose is consistently wordy and diction or tone is inappropriate. Spelling errors are frequent enough to be a distraction.	The essay displays simplistic or inaccurate word choice, monotonous or fragmented sentence structure, and repeated errors in grammar and usage that cause confusion or even render portions of the essay incomprehensible.

Proofreading the Draft

Proofreading is key to providing your audience with a pleasurable reading experience. But proofreading your own writing can be difficult because you may be too close to the writing to see errors. Whenever possible, set your work aside for a day or even an hour, and use one or more of the suggestions below to help you proofread effectively:

- Run the spell checker and carefully consider every suggestion. **Do not automatically accept the suggestions!** Remember that spell checkers cannot identify problems with homonyms (words that sound alike: *too*, *to*, *two*), proper nouns (such as *Detroit* or *Jesse*), or incorrect words (*pubic* for *public*, for example), so check the spelling of these words yourself. Create a checklist of words you've misspelled. Use the checklist to identify and correct words that give you trouble.
- Read your essay aloud slowly. Note and correct any issues that you find. Pay attention to sentences you stumble over; stumbling may be a clue that the sentence is problematic.
- Read your essay from end to beginning, starting with the final sentence and then moving backwards to the sentence just before it. Look for repeated words and similar mistakes that are easy to miss in work that is very familiar.

When your essay is as error free and professional as you can make it, submit it.

PART THREE

Additional Tools and Practice

13

Sentence Guides for Academic Writers

Being a college student means being a college writer. No matter what field you are studying, your instructors will ask you to make sense of what you are learning through writing. When you work on writing assignments in college, you are, in most cases, being asked to write for an academic audience.

Writing academically means thinking academically – asking a lot of questions, digging into the ideas of others, and entering into scholarly debates and academic conversations. As a college writer, you will be asked to read different kinds of texts; understand and evaluate authors' ideas, arguments, and methods; and contribute your own ideas. In this way, you present yourself as a participant in an academic conversation.

What does it mean to be part of an *academic conversation*? Well, think of it this way: You and your friends may have an ongoing debate about the best film trilogy of all time. During your conversations with one another, you analyze the details of the films, introduce points you want your friends to consider, listen to their ideas, and perhaps cite what the critics have said about a particular trilogy. This kind of conversation is not unlike what happens among scholars in academic writing – except they could be debating the best public policy for a social problem or the most promising new theory in treating disease.

If you are uncertain about what academic writing *sounds like* or if you're not sure you're any good at it, this chapter offers guidance for you at the sentence level. It helps answer questions such as these:

How can I present the ideas of others in a way that demonstrates my understanding of the debate?

How can I agree with someone, but add a new idea?

How can I disagree with a scholar without seeming, well, rude?

How can I make clear in my writing which ideas are mine and which ideas are someone else's?

The following sections offer sentence guides for you to use and adapt to your own writing situations. As with all writing that you do, you will have to think about your purpose (reason for writing) and your audience (readers) before knowing which guides will be most appropriate for a particular piece of writing or for a certain part of your essay.

The guides are organized to help you present background information, the views and claims of others, and your own views and claims—all in the context of your purpose and audience.

Presenting Information and Others' Views

When you write in academic situations, you may be asked to spend some time giving background information for or setting a context for your main idea or argument. This often requires you to present or summarize what is known or what has already been said in relation to the question you are asking in your writing.

Presenting What Is Known or Assumed

When you write, you will find that you occasionally need to present something that is known, such as a specific fact or a statistic. The following structures are useful when you are providing background information.

- As we know from history, ______________________________.
- X has shown that ______________________________.
- Research by X and Y suggests that ______________________________.
- According to X, ______________________________ percent of are/favor ______________________________.

In other situations, you may need to present information that is assumed or that is conventional wisdom.

- People often believe that ______________________________.
- Conventional wisdom leads us to believe that ______________________________.
- Many Americans share the idea that ______________________________.
- ______________________________ is a widely held belief.

In order to challenge an assumption or a widely held belief, you have to acknowledge it first. Doing so lets your readers believe that you are placing your ideas in an appropriate context.

- Although many people are led to believe X, there is significant benefit to considering the merits of Y.
- College students tend to believe that ______________________________ when, in fact, the opposite is much more likely the case.

Presenting Others' Views

As a writer, you build your own *ethos*, or credibility, by being able to fairly and accurately represent the views of others. As an academic writer, you will be expected to demonstrate your understanding of a text by summarizing the views or arguments of its author(s). To do so, you will use language like the following.

➤ X argues that ______________________.

➤ X emphasizes the need for ______________________.

➤ In this important article, X and Y claim ______________________
______________________.

➤ X endorses ____________ because ____________.

➤ X and Y have recently criticized the idea that ______________________.

➤ ____________, according to X, is the most critical cause of ____________.

Although you will create your own variations of these sentences as you draft and revise, the guides can be useful tools for thinking through how best to present another writer's claim or finding clearly and concisely.

Presenting Direct Quotations

When the exact words of a source are important for accuracy, authority, emphasis, or flavor, you will want to use a direct quotation. Ordinarily, you will present direct quotations with language of your own that suggests how you are using the source.

➤ X characterizes the problem this way: " . . . "

➤ According to X, ______________________ is defined as " . . . "

➤ ". . . ," explains X.

➤ X argues strongly in favor of the policy, pointing out that " . . . "

Note: You will generally cite direct quotations according to the documentation style your readers expect. MLA style, often used in English and in other humanities courses, recommends using the author's name paired with a page number, if there is one. APA style, used in most social sciences, requires the year of publication generally after the mention of the source, with page numbers after the quoted material. In *Chicago* style, used in history and in some humanities courses, writers use superscript numbers (like this[6]) to refer readers to footnotes or endnotes. In-text citations, like the ones shown below, refer readers to entries in the works cited or reference list.

MLA Lazarín argues that our overreliance on testing in K-12 schools "does not put students first" (20).

APA Lazarín (2014) argues that our overreliance on testing in K-12 schools "does not put students first." (p. 20)

Chicago Lazarín argues that our overreliance on testing in K-12 schools "does not put students first."[6]

Many writers use direct quotations to advance an argument of their own:

Student writer's idea

Standardized testing makes it easier for administrators to measure student performance, but it may not be the best way to measure it. Too much testing wears students out and communicates the idea that recall is the most important skill we want them to develop.

Source's idea

Even education policy advisor Melissa Lazarín argues that our overreliance on testing in K-12 schools "does not put students first" (20).

Presenting Alternative Views

Most debates, whether they are scholarly or popular, are complex—often with more than two sides to an issue. Sometimes you will have to synthesize the views of multiple participants in the debate before you introduce your own ideas.

- On the one hand, X reports that __________, but on the other hand, Y insists that __________.
- Even though X endorses the policy, Y refers to it as "..."
- X, however, isn't convinced and instead argues __________.
- X and Y have supported the theory in the past, but new research by Z suggests that __________.

Presenting Your Own Views

When you write for an academic audience, you will indeed have to demonstrate that you are familiar with the views of others who are asking the same kinds of questions as you are. Much writing that is done for academic purposes asks you to put your arguments in the context of existing arguments—in a way asking you to connect the known to the new.

When you are asked to write a summary or an informative text, your own views and arguments are generally not called for. However, much of the writing you will be assigned to do in college asks you to take a persuasive stance and present a reasoned argument—at times in response to a single text, and at other times in response to multiple texts.

Presenting Your Own Views: Agreement and Extension

Sometimes you agree with the author of a source.

- X's argument is convincing because __________.
- Because X's approach is so __________, it is the best way to __________.

- ➤ X makes an important point when she says ________________.

Other times you find you agree with the author of a source, but you want to extend the point or go a bit deeper in your own investigation. In a way, you acknowledge the source for getting you so far in the conversation, but then you move the conversation along with a related comment or finding.

- ➤ X's proposal for ________________ is indeed worth considering. Going one step further, ________________.
- ➤ X makes the claim that ________________. By extension, isn't it also true, then, that ________________?
- ➤ ________________ has been adequately explained by X. Now, let's move beyond that idea and ask whether ________________.

Presenting Your Own Views: Queries and Skepticism

You may be intimidated when you're asked to talk back to a source, especially if the source is a well-known scholar or expert or even just a frequent voice in a particular debate. College-level writing asks you to be skeptical, however, and approach academic questions with the mind of an investigator. It is acceptable to doubt, to question, to challenge—because the end result is often new knowledge or new understanding about a subject.

- ➤ Couldn't it also be argued that ________________?
- ➤ But is everyone willing to agree that this is the case?
- ➤ While X insists that ________________ is so, he is perhaps asking the wrong question to begin with.
- ➤ The claims that X and Y have made, while intelligent and well-meaning, leave many unconvinced because they have failed to consider ________________.

Presenting Your Own Views: Disagreement or Correction

You may find that at times the only response you have to a text or to an author is complete disagreement.

- ➤ X's claims about ________________ are completely misguided.
- ➤ X presents a long metaphor comparing ________________ to ________________; in the end, the comparison is unconvincing because ________________.

It can be tempting to disregard a source completely if you detect a piece of information that strikes you as false or that you know to be untrue.

- ➤ Although X reports that ________________, recent studies indicate that is not the case.

A NOTE ABOUT USING THE FIRST PERSON ("I")

Some disciplines look favorably upon the use of the first person "I" in academic writing. Others do not and instead stick to using third person. If you are given a writing assignment for a class, you are better off asking your instructor what is preferred or reading through any samples given than *guessing* what might be expected.

First person (I, me, my, we, us, our)

> I question Heddinger's methods and small sample size.
>
> Harnessing children's technology obsession in the classroom is, I believe, the key to improving learning.
>
> Lanza's interpretation focuses on circle imagery as symbolic of the family; my analysis leads me in a different direction entirely.
>
> We would, in fact, benefit from looser laws about farming on our personal property.

Third person (names and other nouns)

> Heddinger's methods and small sample size are questionable.
>
> Harnessing children's technology obsession in the classroom is the key to improving learning.
>
> Lanza's interpretation focuses on circle imagery as symbolic of the family; other readers' analyses may point in a different direction entirely.
>
> Many Americans would, in fact, benefit from looser laws about farming on personal property.

You may feel that not being able to use "I" in an essay in which you present your ideas about a topic is unfair or will lead to weaker statements. Know that you can make a strong argument even if you write in the third person.

➤ While X and Y insist that ____________ is so, an examination of their figures shows that they have made an important miscalculation.

Presenting and Countering Objections to Your Argument

Effective college writers know that their arguments are stronger when they can anticipate objections that others might make.

➤ Some will object to this proposal on the grounds that ____________.

➤ Not everyone will embrace ____________; they may argue instead that ____________.

Countering, or responding to, opposing voices fairly and respectfully strengthens your writing and your *ethos*, or credibility.

➤ X and Y might contend that this interpretation is faulty; however, ____________.

➤ Most ____________ believe that there is too much risk in this approach. But what they have failed to take into consideration is ____________.

Persuading by Putting It All Together

Readers of academic writing often want to know what's at stake in a particular debate or text. They want to know why it is that they should care and keep reading. Aside from crafting individual sentences, you must, of course, keep the bigger picture in mind as you attempt to persuade, inform, evaluate, or review.

Presenting Stakeholders

When you write, you may be doing so as a member of a group affected by the research conversation you have entered. For example, you may be among the thousands of students in your state whose level of debt may change as a result of new laws about financing a college education. In this case, you are a *stakeholder* in the matter. In other words, you have an interest in the matter as a person who could be impacted by the outcome of a decision. On the other hand, you may be writing as an investigator of a topic that interests you but that you aren't directly connected with. You may be persuading your audience on behalf of a group of interested stakeholders – a group of which you yourself are not a member.

You can give your writing some teeth if you make it clear who is being affected by the discussion of the issue and the decisions that have been or will be made about the issue. The groups of stakeholders are highlighted in the following sentences.

- Viewers of Kurosawa's films may not agree with X that ________.
- The research will come as a surprise to parents of children with Type 1 diabetes.
- X's claims have the power to offend potentially every low-wage earner in the state.
- Marathoners might want to reconsider their training regimen if stories such as those told by X and Y are validated by the medical community.

Presenting the "So What"

For readers to be motivated to read your writing, they have to feel as if you're addressing something that matters to them, or something that matters very much to you, or something that should matter to us all. Good academic writing often hooks readers with a sense of urgency – a serious response to a reader's "So what?"

- Having a frank discussion about ________ now will put us in a far better position to deal with ________ in the future. If we are unwilling or unable to do so, we risk ________.
- Such a breakthrough will affect ________ in three significant ways.
- It is easy to believe that the stakes aren't high enough to be alarming; in fact, ________ will be affected by ________.

➤ Widespread disapproval and censorship of such fiction/films/art will mean ______________ for us in the future. Culture should represent ______________.

➤ ______________ could bring about unprecedented opportunities for ______________ to participate in ______________, something never seen before.

➤ New experimentation in ______________ could allow scientists to investigate ______________ in ways they couldn't have imagined ______________ years ago.

Presenting the Players and Positions in a Debate

Some disciplines ask writers to compose a review of the literature as a part of a larger project – or sometimes as a free-standing assignment. In a review of the literature, the writer sets forth a research question, summarizes the key sources that have addressed the question, puts the current research in the context of other voices in the research conversation, and identifies any gaps in the research.

Writing that presents a debate, its players, and their positions can often be lengthy. What follows, however, can give you the sense of the flow of ideas and turns in such a piece of writing.

Student writer states the problem.

Student writer summarizes the views of others on the topic.

Student writer presents her view in the context of current research.

______________ affects more than 30% of children in America, and signs point to a worsening situation in years to come because of A, B, and C. Solutions to the problem have eluded even the sharpest policy minds and brightest researchers. In an important 2003 study, W found that ______________, which pointed to more problems than solutions. [. . .] Research by X and Y made strides in our understanding of ______________ but still didn't offer specific strategies for children and families struggling to ______________. [. . .] When Z rejected both the methods and the findings of X and Y, arguing that ______________, policymakers and health care experts were optimistic. [. . .] *Too much discussion of ______________, however, and too little discussion of ______________, may lead us to solutions that are ultimately too expensive to sustain.*

Using Appropriate Signal Verbs

Verbs matter Using a variety of verbs in your sentences can add strength and clarity as you present others' views and your own views.

WHEN YOU WANT TO PRESENT A VIEW FAIRLY NEUTRALLY

acknowledges	observes
adds	points out
admits	reports
comments	suggests
contends	writes
notes	

➤ X points out that the plan had unintended outcomes.

WHEN YOU WANT TO PRESENT A STRONGER VIEW

argues
asserts
declares
emphasizes
insists

➤ Y argues in favor of a ban on ____________; but Z insists the plan is misguided.

WHEN YOU WANT TO SHOW AGREEMENT

agree
confirms
endorses

➤ An endorsement of X's position is smart for a number of reasons.

WHEN YOU WANT TO SHOW CONTRAST OR DISAGREEMENT

compares
denies
disputes
refutes
rejects

➤ The town must come together and reject X's claims that ____________ is in the best interest of the citizens.

WHEN YOU WANT TO ANTICIPATE AN OBJECTION

admits
acknowledges
concedes

➤ Y admits that closer study of ____________, with a much larger sample size, is necessary for ____________.

14

Editing Practice

Editing Sentences with Boundary Issues

For help identifying and correcting errors with boundary issues, such as sentence fragments, fused (or run-on) sentences, and comma splices, see section S, Sentence Boundaries (pp. H-5 through H-9), in *The St. Martin's Guide to Writing* handbook.

Fragments Correct any fragments in the following sentences. Some sentences may be correct as written.

EXAMPLE:

➤ Among the many art thefts around the world~~. The~~ *, the* Gardner Museum heist stands out.

1. Early in the morning on March 18, 1990. Thieves rang the bell of the Gardner Museum in Boston.
2. The thieves were dressed as police officers. Which convinced a guard to let them in.
3. The two guards were handcuffed and trussed up in the museum's basement.
4. Eighty-one minutes later. The thieves made off with thirteen valuable works of art.
5. Among the works of art stolen. Rembrandt's only known seascape and "The Concert," a priceless painting by Vermeer.

Fused (Run-On) Sentences and Comma Splices Correct any run-on sentences and comma splices in the following sentences. Some sentences may be correct as written.

EXAMPLE:

➤ With more than thirty roles on Broadway, Chita Rivera has become an institution; she has been in show business for over six decades.

1. Rivera began as a ballet dancer a teacher picked her to audition for a place in the prestigious George Balanchine School of American Ballet.
2. At age eighteen Rivera accompanied a friend to a Broadway audition imagine her friend's distress when Rivera got the part.
3. The talented dancer won roles in many Broadway musicals, it was *West Side Story* that made her a star.
4. She played Anita. A Puerto Rican girl from the Upper West Side of New York.
5. It wasn't Rivera who played Anita in the film version of the musical. Rita Moreno got the part.

Editing Sentences with Grammatical Issues

For help identifying and correcting grammatical issues, see section G, Grammatical Sentences (pp. H-10 through H-26), in *The St. Martin's Guide to Writing* handbook.

Pronoun Reference Correct any instances of vague or unclear pronoun references in the following sentences.

EXAMPLE:

➤ The school's principal wanted to meet with my father before ~~he~~ *my father* spoke to me.

1. The principal knows that many students feel distrust of the administration, which is not good for the school.
2. In child psychology, they say that a student's dislike of school can be grounded in fear.
3. Administrators provide students with many opportunities for positive experiences, but they could not care less.
4. If students expect administrators to be mean, it will not surprise them.
5. Cynicism about the commitment of educators may lead to apathy, and it can spread like measles.

Pronoun Agreement Correct any errors in pronoun-antecedent agreement in the following sentences. Some sentences may be correct as written.

EXAMPLE:

➤ Seismology, the science of earthquakes, ~~have their~~ *has its* own measurement system, the Richter scale.

1. Human lives is valuable, and more could be saved if earthquakes were predictable.
2. Seismology has made many advances in the past few decades, but they still cannot predict when an earthquake will occur.
3. A magnitude 10 earthquake would cause movement of the earth for an hour.
4. Seismologists cannot predict just how strong any earthquake will be before they happen.
5. People who live in a seismic zone should always know where the safest place in his or her home is.

Subject–Verb Agreement Correct subject–verb agreement in the following sentences. Some sentences may be correct as written.

EXAMPLE:

➤ In ancient Greece, sneezing ~~were~~ *was* considered a good omen.

1. The early Romans, in contrast, believed that sneezing was a sign of the plague.
2. When the bubonic plague swept Europe, Pope Gregory supposedly suggest that people bless themselves for protection.
3. Americans reflect a shared past with medieval Europe by saying "God bless you" when someone sneeze.
4. Many people in East Asia believes that sneezing means someone is talking behind your back.
5. In a pre-scientific era, this kind of superstition were a way for people to exercise control over their fates.

Misplaced or Dangling Modifiers Correct any misplaced or dangling modifiers in the following sentences. Some sentences may be correct as written. **Note:** The passage can be edited in more than one way.

EXAMPLE:

➤ *Elephants' ability* ~~Providing many important benefits, elephants must be able~~ to communicate with each other over long distances *provides them with many important benefits*.

1. Knowing how far a communication can be heard, the ability is crucial in letting an elephant know how large its group's territory might be.
2. After finding a new source of food, information can be transmitted to others in the group without leaving the spot.

3. When available for mating, sounds can signal mature males that females are also ready for reproduction.
4. Considering all these factors, a widely scattered group of elephants is essential for good communications.
5. Virtually the same as belonging, a strongly social creature needs to communicate.

Editing Sentences with Stylistic Issues

For help identifying and correcting stylistic issues, see sections E, Effective Sentences (pp. H-27 through H-42), and W, Word Choice (pp. H-43 through H-50), in *The St. Martin's Guide to Writing* handbook.

Wordiness Rewrite the passage below to make it more concise. The passage can be edited in more than one way.

EXAMPLE:

➤ On ~~the day of~~ August 28, 1963, 250,000 people ~~—that is to say, a quarter of a million people—marched on~~ ^*convened in* Washington, D.C. ^*for* ~~This was a march that what was called~~ the March on Washington for Jobs and Freedom.

Those crowded around the Lincoln Memorial, the memorial built to honor U.S. president Abraham Lincoln, who was known as the "Great Emancipator," and the site for the rally on that day and time, and those who heard the rally's speakers on radio stations and television stations in New York, Kansas, Texas, California, Delaware, Pennsylvania, and so many other states, were witness to one of the most famous speeches in American history at that time or any time. It was given by thirty-four-year-old Martin Luther King, a young minister and the head of the Southern Christian Leadership Conference, which helped organize the march on Washington on that August day. King was the final speaker on a long, long list that included politicians, labor leaders, and community activists, all people who had an interest in jobs, freedom, and civil rights. "I have a dream," King said, beginning to improvise or depart from his prepared speech as he warmed to his crowd and his message, "that one day this nation will rise up and live out the true meaning of its creed: 'We hold these truths to be self-evident, that all men are created equal.'" As a matter of fact, as King continued his speech, speaking to the crowd, he started weaving the phrase "I have a dream" in and out of his speech, the oration that was the last on a long day of speeches. The crowd became very stirred up, very emotional, holding hands with each other, and weeping and crying out loud. For the first time ever in American history, a large white audience listened to the voice of a black man poetically demanding such important things as justice, freedom, and a future in which his children could "live in a nation where they will not be judged by the color of their skin but by the content of their character." At the end of this important, groundbreaking speech, which was the first of its kind to reach a wide audience of majority and minority people, King cried out, "Free at last, free at last, thank God almighty, we are free at last!" The crowd let out a mighty cry that sounded like thunder or the skies opening.

Parallelism Problems Correct any errors in parallelism in the following sentences. Some sentences may be correct as written.

EXAMPLE:

➤ When Amber goes to the grocery store, she is provisioning more than ~~she shops~~ ^*shopping*.

She makes sure to get necessities like milk, cereal, and a dozen eggs, but she gets three of everything. I have tried asking her politely either to cut back on what she buys or to shop less frequently. I suppose it would be all right if we had unlimited storage space, sprinters' metabolisms, or if guests regularly visited. From Amber's point of view, it is better to have a lot of extra food than running out. I joke with her that she likes shopping better than going on vacation. She doesn't laugh but instead suggests that I try living in a home with no shoppers and no "magic elves" to fill the cupboards. Then, I tell Amber I mean to neither hurt her feelings nor to insult her for her good deeds. I thank her for being a conscientious roommate, and she's a good friend. Then we cook up a dozen eggs, a family-size box of macaroni and cheese, or a box of pancakes.

Problems with Word Choice

Inappropriate Diction

Edit the following paragraph for appropriate diction and connotation. Assume an academic audience.

EXAMPLE:

➤ Very few ~~critters~~ *mammals* in North America truly hibernate.

To hibernate, a creature must drop its body temperature, as well as its respiration and heart rate. True hibernators must also develop a layer of fat that will provide energy during the long sleep. A woodchuck, for example, has all four of these characteristics. While it's catching some z's, its body temperature falls almost 50 degrees, and it breathes about once every four minutes. Its heart rate slacks off, and while sleeping, it feeds off the lard stored in its body.

Many of the mammals that are described as hibernating are actually in torpor, a state that might be considered hibernation lite. These animals can get up to hunt for snacks, something a true hibernator cannot do. Many animals in torpor cannot risk lowering their body rates as much as the true hibernators do. Black bears, chipmunks, and raccoons are all examples of animals that enter torpor rather than hibernation.

Inexact Words

Replace inexact words with words that more precisely fit the context. Assume an academic audience.

EXAMPLE:

➤ Even though the influenza epidemic of 1918 killed 20 million people around the world, many students never learn about the ~~debacle~~ *tragedy*.

One excuse for why the epidemic has been overlooked is that it overlapped with the last months of World War I. The symptoms of the 1918 influenza were not the same as the everyday flu that kills thirty-six thousand Americans each year. The body aches, fever, and nausea typically associated with flu seem gentle compared with those of the 1918 influenza. Victims of the 1918 influenza often bled from their noses, throats, and eyes, and their skin color darkened a lot.

Some epidemiologists who have studied the 1918 influenza believe that the epidemic should have been described by a much scarier name: plague. Just the sound of the word entails images of the bubonic plague, also known as "The Black Death," which conquered Asia and Europe in the fourteenth century, killing possibly up to one-quarter of the population, according to some historians. Like the 1918 influenza epidemic, the bubonic plague is also little heeded today. In fact, few people realize that the children's game "ring-around-the rosy" refers to the symptoms of the plague, the actions people took to ward off the symptoms, and the nasty fate of many of the victims.

Biased Language
Replace words that suggest bias with more neutral ones.

EXAMPLE:

➤ During World War II many American ~~girls~~ *women* joined the war effort by going to work in munitions plants, taking the place of the men who were fighting in ~~the Old World~~ *Europe* and the ~~Orient~~ *Pacific*.

While these girls worked in numerous positions, collectively they became known as "Rosie the Riveters." The Rosies were made famous in two works of art that depicted the gentler sex in extremely different ways. Famous illustrator Norman Rockwell depicted his Rosie on the cover of the May 29, 1943, issue of the *Saturday Evening Post* magazine. His Rosie is no runway babe; she looks like the lady next door. She wears mannish blue jeans with rolled-up cuffs. Her rivet gun rests on her lap while she munches on a sandwich. Her goggles are pushed up onto her forehead, where a rag ties up her hair. She seems oblivious to the huge American flag waving in the background. J. Howard Miller's model in the famous "Rosie the Riveter: We Can Do It" poster is very aware of the viewer, and he is very aware of her. She's a dish, for one thing. Her dark curls peek out from under a stylish red polka-dot kerchief as she looks straight at the viewer. She has rolled up her spotless, trim blue shirt to show off her muscles. The machinery she operates is nowhere in sight. Given that she is wearing heavy false eyelashes and thick lipstick and has polished nails, it's hard to believe that this little miss ever did a day's work, but she kept up the morale of the boys abroad and inspired gals at home to take on new roles.

Strong, Active Verbs
Replace passive verbs with strong, active verbs.

EXAMPLE:

Scientists have discovered
➤ ~~S~~ome intriguing facts about insect flight ~~have been discovered by scientists~~.

Active flight was first evolved by insects. The most diverse wing structures of any flying animals are had by insects. The flight muscles of insects demonstrate the highest-known metabolic rate of any animal structure. Insect flight is being studied by a team of biologists at the University of California, Berkeley. Models based on airplane flight could not be used by them. Insects flap and rotate their wings up to six hundred times per second. Complicated airflow patterns are created by this continual motion. These airflow patterns cannot be analyzed thoroughly by scientists. An accurate model of an insect in flight could be used by engineers to develop tiny helicopters for environmental monitoring or surveillance purposes.

15

Possible Answers to Activities in Chapter 14, "Editing Practice"

Editing Sentences with Boundary Issues

Fragments

1. Early in the morning on March 18, 1990, thieves rang the bell of the Gardner Museum in Boston.
2. The thieves were dressed as police officers, which convinced a guard to let them in.
3. Correct
4. Eighty-one minutes later, the thieves made off with thirteen valuable works of art.
5. Among the works of art stolen were Rembrandt's only known seascape and "The Concert," a priceless painting by Vermeer.

Fused (Run-On) Sentences and Comma Splices

1. Rivera began as a ballet dancer, after a teacher picked her to audition for a place in the prestigious George Balanchine School of American Ballet.
2. At age eighteen, Rivera accompanied a friend to a Broadway audition. Imagine her friend's distress when Rivera got the part.
3. The talented dancer won roles in many Broadway musicals, but it was *West Side Story* that made her a star.
4. She played Anita, a Puerto Rican girl from the Upper West Side of New York.
5. Correct

Editing Sentences with Grammatical Issues

Pronoun Reference

1. The principal knows that many students feel distrust of the administration, and this attitude is not good for the school.
2. Child psychologists say that a student's dislike of school can be grounded in fear.
3. Administrators provide students with many opportunities for positive experiences, but students could not care less.
4. If students expect administrators to be mean, an administrator's hostility will not surprise them.
5. Cynicism about the commitment of educators may lead to apathy, which can spread like measles.

Pronoun Agreement

1. Human life is valuable, and more lives could be saved if earthquakes were predictable.
2. Seismologists have made many advances in the past few decades, but they still cannot predict when an earthquake will occur.
3. Correct
4. Seismologists cannot predict just how strong any earthquake will be before it happens.
5. People who live in a seismic zone should always know where the safest place in their home is.

Subject–Verb Agreement

1. Correct
2. When the bubonic plague swept Europe, Pope Gregory supposedly **suggested** that people bless themselves for protection.
3. Americans reflect a shared past with medieval Europe by saying "God bless you" when someone **sneezes**.
4. Many people in East Asia **believe** that sneezing means someone is talking behind your back.
5. In a pre-scientific era, this kind of superstition **was** a way for people to exercise control.

Misplaced or Dangling Modifiers

1. Knowing how far a communication can be heard gives an elephant crucial information about how large its group's territory might be.
2. After finding a new source of food, an elephant can transmit this information to others in the group without leaving the spot.

3. Females that are available for mating can use sounds to signal mature males that are also ready for reproduction.
4. Considering all these factors, good communications are essential to a widely scattered group of elephants.
5. To such a strongly social creature, communicating is virtually the same as belonging.

Editing Sentences with Stylistic Issues

Wordiness

Note: The passage below can be edited in more than one way.

On August 28, 1963, 250,000 people convened in Washington, D.C. for the March on Washington for Jobs and Freedom. The marchers who crowded around the Lincoln Memorial (built to honor the U.S. president known as the "Great Emancipator"), and those who heard the rally's speakers on radio and television stations across the United States, were witness to one of the most famous speeches in American history. It was given by thirty-four-year-old Martin Luther King, a young minister and the head of the Southern Christian Leadership Conference, which helped to organize the march. King was the final speaker on a long list that included politicians, labor leaders, and community activists. "I have a dream," King said, beginning to depart from his prepared speech as he warmed to his crowd and his message, "that one day this nation will rise up and live out the true meaning of its creed: 'We hold these truths to be self-evident, that all men are created equal.'" As King continued speaking to the crowd, he started weaving the phrase "I have a dream" into his speech. The crowd became stirred up, holding hands and crying out loud. For the first time in American history, a large white audience listened to a black man poetically demanding justice, freedom, and a future in which his children could "live in a nation where they will not be judged by the color of their skin but by the content of their character." At the end of this groundbreaking speech, King cried out, "Free at last, free at last, thank God almighty, we are free at last!" The crowd let out a mighty cry that sounded like thunder.

Parallelism Problems

Note: The passage below can be edited in more than one way.

When Amber goes to the grocery store, she is provisioning more than shopping. She makes sure to get necessities like milk, cereal, and eggs, but she gets three of everything. I have tried asking her politely either to cut back on what she buys or to shop less frequently. [no change] I suppose it would be all right if we had unlimited storage space, sprinters' metabolisms, or regular guests. From Amber's point of view, it is better to have a lot of extra food than to risk running out. I joke with her that she likes shopping better than going on vacation. [no change] She doesn't laugh but instead suggests that I try living in a home with no shoppers and no "magic elves" to fill the cupboards. [no change] Then, I tell Amber I mean neither to hurt her feelings nor to insult her for her good deeds. I thank her for being a conscientious roommate and a good friend. Then we cook up a dozen eggs, a family-size box of macaroni and cheese, or a box of pancakes. [no change]

Problems with Word Choice

Note: The passages below can be edited in more than one way.

Inappropriate Diction
Very few mammals in North America truly hibernate. To hibernate, a creature must drop its body temperature, as well as its respiration and heart rate. True hibernators must also develop a layer of fat that will provide energy during the long sleep. A woodchuck, for example, has all four of these characteristics. While it's **sleeping,** its body temperature falls almost 50 degrees, and it breathes about once every four minutes. Its heart rate **slows**, and while sleeping, it feeds off the **fat** stored in its body.

Many of the mammals that are described as hibernating are actually in torpor, a state that might be considered **a less complete form of** hibernation. These animals **awaken** to hunt for **food**, something a true hibernator cannot do. Many animals in torpor cannot risk lowering their body rates as much as the true hibernators do. Black bears, chipmunks, and raccoons are all examples of animals that enter torpor rather than hibernate.

Inexact Words
Even though the influenza epidemic of 1918 killed 20 million people around the world, many students never learn about the **tragedy**. One **explanation** for why the epidemic has been overlooked is that it overlapped with the last months of World War I. The symptoms of the 1918 influenza were not the same as the **common** flu that kills thirty-six thousand Americans each year. The body aches, fever, and nausea typically associated with flu seem **mild** compared with those of the 1918 influenza. Victims of the 1918 influenza often bled from their noses, throats, and eyes, and their skin color darkened **considerably**.

Some epidemiologists who have studied the 1918 influenza believe that the epidemic should have been called by a much **more emphatic** name: plague. Just the sound of the word **evokes** images of the bubonic plague, also known as "The Black Death," which **devastated** Asia and Europe in the fourteenth century, killing possibly up to one-quarter of the population, according to some historians. Like the 1918 influenza epidemic, the bubonic plague is also little **known** today. In fact, few people realize that the children's game "ring-around-the rosy" refers to the symptoms of the plague, the actions people took to ward off the symptoms, and the **horrible** fate of many of the victims.

Biased Language
During World War II many American **women** joined the war effort by going to work in munitions plants, taking the place of the men who were fighting in **Europe** and the **Pacific.** While these **women** worked in numerous positions, collectively they became known as "Rosie the Riveters." The Rosies were made famous in two works of art that depicted **women** in extremely different ways. Famous illustrator Norman Rockwell depicted his Rosie on the cover of the May 29, 1943, issue of the *Saturday Evening Post*

magazine. His Rosie is no **fashion model**; she looks like the **woman** next door. She wears **blue jeans** with rolled-up cuffs. Her rivet gun rests on her lap while she munches on a sandwich. Her goggles are pushed up onto her forehead, where a rag ties up her hair. She seems oblivious to the huge American flag waving in the background. J. Howard Miller's model in the famous "Rosie the Riveter: We Can Do It" poster is very aware of the viewer, and **he or she** is very aware of her. She's **an attractive woman**, for one thing. Her dark curls peak out from under a stylish red polka-dot kerchief as she looks straight at the viewer. She has rolled up her spotless, trim blue shirt to show off her muscles. The machinery she operates is nowhere in sight. Given that she is wearing heavy false eyelashes and thick lipstick and has polished nails, it's hard to believe that this **woman** ever did a day's work, but she kept up the morale of the **soldiers** abroad and inspired **women** at home to take on new roles.

Strong, Active Verbs

Scientists have discovered some intriguing facts about insect flight. Insects were the first animals to evolve active flight. Insects have the most diverse wing structure of any flying animals. The flight muscles of insects demonstrate the highest-known metabolic rate of any animal structure. [no change] A team of scientists at the University of California, Berkeley, is studying insect flight. They cannot use models based on airplane flight. Insects flap and rotate their wings up to six hundred times per second. [no change] This continual motion creates complicated airflow patterns. Scientists cannot thoroughly analyze these airflow patterns. Scientists could use an accurate model of insects in flight to develop tiny helicopters for environmental monitoring or surveillance purposes.